Stand United in Joy

An Exposition of Philippians

ROBERT G. GROMACKI

Baker Book House
Grand Rapids, Michigan 49506

PHOTOLITHOPRINTED BY CUSHING - MALLOY, INC.
ANN ARBOR, MICHIGAN, UNITED STATES OF AMERICA

To

Cedarville College

Chancellor James T. Jeremiah
President Paul Dixon
Dean Clifford Johnson
and the

Bible Department Faculty

Mead Armstrong
Richard Durham
Jean Fisher
James Grier
George Lawlor
Richard McIntosh
Donald Parvin
Jack Riggs
David Warren

Contents

Preface

Division and anxiety mark the church of Jesus Christ today. Denominations, churches, families, and individuals are fragmented, confused, and depressed. A revival of unity and joy is needed, but it must first begin in the heart of a yielded believer. In the first century the same situation prevailed in the church at Philippi. Paul wrote this epistle to produce a oneness of joy within the members of that assembly. In our contemporary society, a fresh study of this epistle is needed by each Christian. Do you have inner joy? Are you humble? Do you believe that God is in control? Study Philippians with the aid of this book, and let God transform your heart and mind.

This study has been designed to teach the Word of God to others. It is an attempt to make clear the meaning of the English text (King James Version) through organization, exposition, and careful usage of the Greek text. It is planned as a readable study through a nontechnical vocabulary with a smooth transition from one section to the next. The words of the English Bible are isolated by quotation marks within the book, the Greek words are transliterated, and necessary grammatical explanations have been put into the footnotes.

Divided into thirteen chapters, it can be used by adult Sunday school classes or Bible study groups for a traditional quarter of thirteen weeks. Concluding each chapter are discussion questions, designed to stimulate personal inquiry and to make the truth of God relevant. This book can also be used by one person as a private Bible study guide. In either case, this exposition should be read with an open Bible. It is my prayer that men and women will be blessed and edified as they undertake this study of Philippians.

A special word of thanks is extended to Cornelius Zylstra and Dan Van't Kerkhoff, editors of Baker Book House, who encouraged and assisted me in this project. This volume will complement my other expositions in this series: *Called to be Saints* (I Corinthians), *Stand Firm in the Faith* (II Corinthians), and *Stand Fast in Liberty* (Galatians).

Also, my love and appreciation go to my wife, Gloria, and to my daughter, Gail, who both carefully typed the manuscript.

Introduction

I. WRITER

The contents of the Epistle strongly support the traditional view that Paul wrote this book. First of all, he calls himself "Paul" (1:1). Not only is Timothy closely associated with him in the ministry, but Paul regarded him as his son (1:1; 2:19–23; cf. I Tim. 1:2). The reference to Timothy is significant because he was on the missionary team, along with Paul, that originally evangelized Philippi (Acts 16). The biographical background of the author (3:4–6) harmonizes with the details of Paul's life as recorded in the other Pauline letters and in Acts. The historical background for the writing of the letter fits into Paul's known life. He was in prison, probably in Rome (1:7, 13), but he expected to be released and to revisit Philippi (1:25, 27; 2:24; cf. I Tim. 1:3).

II. CITY OF PHILIPPI

The city was located on a fertile plain about nine miles from the Aegean Sea, northwest of the island of Thasos. Neapolis served as its seaport. In New Testament times it was regarded as "the chief city of that part of Macedonia, and a colony" (Acts 16:12), but Thessalonica was actually the capital of the Roman province. Its inhabitants were Roman citizens, who had the rights not only to vote but also to govern themselves. It is probable that they were quite anti-Semitic since no Jewish synagogue was constructed in this city, although large numbers of Jews were found in other Greek cities (Thessalonica, Berea, Athens, and Corinth).

Its history is interesting. Originally, it was a Phoenician mining town because of its proximity to gold mines located in the mountains and on the island of Thasos. Later, Philip of Macedon, the father of Alexander the Great, took the city from the empire of Thrace and renamed it after himself.[1] Still later, a crucial battle between the coalition of Octavius and Antony and that of Brutus and Cassius was fought there. The former won, thus ending the Roman republic in 42 B.C. As a Roman colony, the city grew in prominence because it was on the main road from Rome to the province of Asia.

Today the city lies in ruins. The site has been excavated by archaeologists who have uncovered a marketplace, the foundation of a large arched gateway, and an amphitheater dating back to Roman times.

III. ESTABLISHMENT OF THE CHURCH

Soon after Paul and Silas started out on Paul's second missionary journey, they recruited Timothy to assist them (Acts 15:36–16:5). Forbidden by the Spirit to preach in Asia and Bithynia, they came to the coastal city of Troas; it was here that "a vision appeared to Paul in the night; There stood a man of Macedonia, and prayed him, saying, Come over into Macedonia, and help us" (Acts 16:9). The missionary team, joined by Luke, sensed that God wanted them to evangelize Macedonia, and so they left for Neapolis the next day. This was the first time that the gospel was brought into Europe.

At Philippi on the Sabbath, they ministered to a group of women (probably Jewesses and Gentile proselytes) by the river, since there was no synagogue in the city. Lydia, a merchant woman of Thyatira, and her household believed and were baptized (Acts 16:15; cf. 16:40).

[1]The Greek word for Philippi means "lover of horses."

10

The next significant event in Philippi occurred when Paul cast out of a slave girl a demonic spirit that enabled the girl to tell fortunes. Her enraged masters seized Paul and Silas,[2] dragged them to the city's rulers, and brought this false accusation against them: "These men, being Jews, do exceedingly trouble our city, and teach customs, which are not lawful for us to receive, neither to observe, being Romans" (Acts 16:20–21). Because of the Roman antagonism toward Jews, the multitude beat them and cast them into prison.

At midnight Paul and Silas prayed and sang, communicating their faith to the other prisoners. An earthquake shook the prison's foundations, opened the doors, and loosed the chains from the walls. The jailor, fearful that the prisoners under his care had fled, was about to commit suicide when Paul stopped him. Paul then led the jailor and his household to a saving knowledge of Christ. At his release the next day, Paul revealed that both he and Silas had Roman citizenship and had been beaten wrongfully. They then went to Lydia's house, ministered to the believers, and left for Thessalonica, leaving Luke behind.[3] The young church at Philippi probably had a strange membership consisting of a converted business woman, a former demonic soothsayer, a jailor, and perhaps some prisoners.

Close contact between Paul and the Philippian church was maintained after this initial contact. The church sent gifts to Paul on two separate occasions during his ministry in Thessalonica (4:14–16; cf. Acts 17:1–9). Silas was probably sent by Paul from Athens to do some additional work there (Acts 17:15–16; I Thess. 3:1–6; cf. Acts 18:5). During his third journey, Paul went into the province of Macedonia, with an obvious stop at Philippi (Acts 20:1); after three months in Corinth, he revisited Macedonia and Philippi be-

[2]Probably the reason Luke and Timothy were not seized was because the former was a pure Gentile and the latter was half Greek.

[3]The first "we" section (Acts 16:10–40) ended here; the narrative reverted to the third person plural, "they"; therefore, the author, Luke, must have stayed in Philippi.

STAND UNITED IN JOY

Paul's Second Missionary Journey

Paul's Third Missionary Journey

fore he left for Jerusalem (Acts 20:2–6). On this final contact
Luke rejoined Paul and accompanied him until the apostle's
martyrdom.[4]

IV. TIME AND PLACE

The complicated background behind the writing of this
epistle can best be illustrated through a series of five direc-
tional arrows:[5]

Paul	1 ⟶	**Church**
in	⟵ 2	**in**
Rome	3 ⟶	**Philippi**
	⟵ 4	
	5 ⟶	

News of Paul's imprisonment in Rome had come to the
Philippian·church by some unknown means, and it created a
great deal of concern and anxiety (arrow 1).

To get firsthand information on Paul's predicament, the
church authorized Epaphroditus to go to Rome to confer with
Paul and to present him a monetary gift for his financial
needs (4:10, 14–18)(arrow 2).

When Epaphroditus saw that Paul's material needs were
much greater than the size of the Philippian gift, he stayed on
in Rome, working to raise more money for Paul (2:25, 30). In
doing this, Epaphroditus became very ill and almost died
(2:27, 30). Word of his severe sickness somehow reached
Philippi and caused a new concern for the church (2:26)
(arrow 3).

The fact that the church knew about his illness reached
Epaphroditus in Rome and became a burden to him (2:26)
(arrow 4).

---

[4]Note the resumption of the "we—us" narrative (Acts 20:5–6) and the
continued usage of it throughout the rest of Acts.

[5]The number of each arrow, enclosed in parentheses, appears after appropriate remarks.

During the time period covered by the third and fourth communications, God had healed Epaphroditus totally, or at least sufficiently so that he was well enough to return to Philippi (2:27). Paul determined then to send Epaphroditus back to Philippi so that the church might rejoice at his return (2:28). The apostle thus used this occasion to write this epistle and to send it to Philippi by way of Epaphroditus (arrow 5). It probably was written near the end of Paul's two years of imprisonment at Rome (A.D. 59–61) because Paul was confident about an imminent acquittal or release (1:25; 2:24).

There has been some thought that Paul wrote this letter from a prison in Ephesus. Some plausible arguments have been set forth for this position. *First,* Paul planned to send Timothy to Philippi, and he did just that from Ephesus (2:19–23; cf. Acts 19:22); but why did Paul not mention Erastus in this epistle if these two sendings of Timothy are identical? *Second,* it is possible that there was a Praetorium guard[6] stationed at Ephesus (1:13) and that "Caesar's household" referred to the imperial civil servants (4:22) located there; but the natural use of those phrases argue for a Roman setting.

Third, it is argued that Luke is not mentioned in Philippians although he was in Rome with Paul and was listed both in Colossians and Philemon. Since Luke was not with Paul in Ephesus (Acts 19), that city seems to be more likely as the place of origin. However, Luke was not mentioned in Ephesians either. Also, if Paul did write from Ephesus, why did he not include the names of those who were with him in that city (e.g., Gaius and Aristarchus [Acts 19:29])?

Fourth, the Ephesian proponents say that too much time would have been involved in the five exchanges of communication; however, it only required a month to travel from Rome to Philippi. These exchanges could have taken place within a six-month period, well within the two-year limits of

---

[6]A better translation for *en tō holō praitōriō* is "among the whole praetorium guard" (soldiers) rather than "in all the palace" (a building).

Paul's Roman imprisonment. Until more objective evidence is forthcoming, the traditional view that Paul wrote from Rome must stand.

V. PURPOSES

Paul learned about the spiritual needs of the church through conversations with Epaphroditus and with those who came to Rome with the report of the church's concern over the illness of Epaphroditus. *First,* Paul wanted to relieve their anxiety over the circumstances of his imprisonment (1:1–30). They thought that the apostle's ministry had been brought to an abrupt stop, but Paul assured them that God was using the episode for the advancement of the gospel. *Second,* there apparently was a growing disunity among the members as evidenced by the fact that Paul appealed to them to manifest humility and unity (2:1–8). *Third,* he wanted to inform them of a possible imminent visit by Timothy (2:18–24). *Fourth,* he attempted to explain the reasons behind Epaphroditus' sickness and healing (2:25–30). *Fifth,* he desired to warn them against the deceitful tactics and doctrines of the Judaizers (3:1–4:1). *Sixth,* he admonished two women, Euodias and Syntyche, to maintain spiritual unity (4:2–3). *Seventh,* he prescribed truth that would give them mental and emotional stability to replace their anxiety (4:4–9). *Eighth,* he wanted to thank them for their financial assistance (4:10–20). *Finally,* he expressed greetings to all of them (4:21–23).

VI. DISTINCTIVE FEATURES

The intimate relationship that existed between Paul and the Philippian church can be seen in his frequent use of the first person singular, personal pronoun. In these four short chapters there are over one hundred occurrences of such words as *I, me,* and *my.* In fact, the word *I* can be found fifty-two times. This does not mean that Paul lacked humility; rather, it shows the natural person-to-person rapport between him and the people. Thus, of all the epistles written to churches, Philippians is the most personal.

Within the book is a strong emphasis upon the word *gospel*, found nine times in various constructions: "fellowship in the gospel" (1:5); "defence and confirmation of the gospel" (1:7); "furtherance of the gospel" (1:12); "defence of the gospel" (1:17); "conversation be as it becometh the gospel of Christ" (1:27a); "faith of the gospel" (1:27b); "served with me in the gospel" (2:22); "laboured with me in the gospel" (4:3); and "beginning of the gospel" (4:15).

This book has a traditional reputation of being the epistle of joy. Various forms of the words *joy* and *rejoice* are found eighteen times in the book. This theme can be seen in the key verse: "Rejoice in the Lord always: and again I say, Rejoice" (4:4).

One of the greatest christological passages occurs within this book (2:5–11) as an example or illustration to the Philippians of genuine humility and obedience. It speaks of Christ's eternal deity, incarnation, humiliation, death, resurrection, and exaltation via ascension. Theologians have called it the *Kenosis passage,* based upon the Greek text underlying the phrase: "But made himself of no reputation" (2:7). The three Greek words of this phrase *(alla heauton ekenōsen)* are literally translated: "But himself he emptied." The Kenosis concept takes its name from a transliteration of the Greek word *ekenōsen.* The question raised is: Of what did Christ empty Himself when He became man? Did He empty Himself of His divine attributes? If He did, then He was less than God when He walked upon the earth. But He was just as much God when He was in the womb of Mary or when He hung on the cross as He was when He created the worlds. Rather, Christ surrendered the independent exercise of His divine attributes when He became incarnate. He had them, but He did not always use them. He learned, hungered, and grew weary; these are characteristics of His human nature. However, He did use His divine attributes at times under the control of the Holy Spirit. He forgave sin, created food, gave life to the dead, and walked on the water. The emptying of

Himself also involved the veiling of the outward display of His deity and glory in human flesh. No halo was upon His head nor did a glow radiate from His face. Only on the Mount of Transfiguration (Matt. 17:1–13) was His glory permitted to shine through His flesh. He also emptied Himself of the prerogative of sovereignty, allowing Himself to be served in order to assume the attitude of a servant to others.

The Book of Philippians also provides an insight into Paul's motivations: "For to me to live is Christ, and to die is gain" (1:21). Just as people think "golf" when the name Arnold Palmer is mentioned, so believers thought "Christ" when Paul's name was spoken. Paul wanted Christ to be magnified in his body, whether through living or dying for Him. He later elaborated upon his goals (3:10–14).

Ruins at Philippi.

1

The Point of Contact
Philippians 1:1–2

.The church at Philippi was anxious over the welfare of
Paul. They were afraid that his ministry might be over and
that he might even be martyred by the Roman government
officials. Their apprehension was heightened by an awareness of the severe illness of their messenger, Epaphroditus.
To them, the entire situation was depressing and deteriorat-
ing. These conditions caused within their own assembly a
fear of persecution (1:28), a spirit of disunity and conflict
(2:2–3; 4:2), an attitude of dissatisfaction (2:14–15), an open-
ness to false teaching (3:2, 17–19), and an anxiety which
promoted emotional and mental instability (4:6–7). They had
slowly lost their spiritual joy (3:1; 4:4).

Paul had to assure them that God was indeed working all
things for the mutual good of the apostle and the church
(Rom. 8:28). Their perspective needed to be changed. They
had to rejoice in unity. How could this transformation take
place? *First,* adverse circumstances had to be viewed as op-
portunities to proclaim the gospel, not as obstacles to personal growth (1:12). *Second,* selfishness had to be replaced
by selflessness (2:4). *Third,* a right relationship to God had to
be established for both salvation and service (3:7–8, 13).
Fourth, thanksgiving and contentment had to replace worry
(4:6, 11–12).

In the above passages, the apostle centered his exposition
around the concept of *things. First,* circumstances were "the
things which happened unto me" (1:12). *Second,* selfishness
occurs when a man looks "on his own things" (2:4).

Third, salvation means that a person regards "what things were gain" to him as loss (3:7); service motivates a believer to reach forth "unto those things which are before" (3:13). *Fourth,* a trusting Christian will be "careful for nothing" (4:6).

The physical recovery of Epaphroditus and his imminent return to Philippi thus provided Paul with an opportunity to inform the church about his inner response to the Roman imprisonment. Both the epistle and the homecoming of their friend were designed to produce a new joy within their hearts.

I. THE SALUTATION (1:1)

The opening remarks contain what is normally found within a Pauline greeting: identification of self, associate, and readers; a blessing; and a prayer of thanksgiving (cf. Rom. 1:1–8; Col. 1:1–3; I Thess. 1:1–2; II Thess. 1:1–3).

A. Author (1:1a)

1. His name

In his pre-Christian life, Paul was known as Saul of Tarsus, the persecutor of the church (Acts 7:58; 8:1, 3; 9:1). When Christ revealed Himself to the young Pharisee, He addressed him as Saul (Acts 9:4). For the next nine years of his Christian life, he maintained the usage of his given name (Acts 9:17, 19, 22, 26; 11:25, 30; 13:1–2).

At the beginning of his first missionary journey, however, he changed his name to Paul (Acts 13:9, 13). On this occasion at Cyprus, Paul demonstrated his apostolic authority for the first time by imposing blindness upon the sorcerer Elymas, who had resisted the gospel witness. Through this miracle, Paul won his first convert, the Roman proconsul Sergius Paulus (Acts 13:7–12). It is plausible that Saul assumed the name of Paul *(Paulos)* as a constant reminder of the grace and power of God who can save sinners and call them to Christian service.[1]

The Latin *paulus* means "little" or "small." Before God, Paul saw himself as "the least of all saints" (Eph. 3:8). Late in life he still viewed himself as the "chief" of sinners (I Tim. 1:15). The new name manifested the change from the pride of Phariseeism to the humility of Christianity.

Born into the Jewish tribe of Benjamin, he was probably named by his parents after the first king of Israel (3:5; cf. I Sam. 9:1–2). King Saul, who was physically tall, was humbled by God because of his pride and arrogant self-will. The proud Pharisee was also humbled by God on the road to Damascus, but he arose to become a dedicated servant of Christ.

2. His associate

His name *(Timotheos)* is based upon a combination of two Greek words, meaning "honor" *(timō)* and "God" *(theos)*. He was one who honored God in his life and who in turn was honored by God. The Lord said to Eli, the judge who guided Samuel: " . . . for them that honor me I will honor" (I Sam. 2:30). Timothy personified that divine decree.

A native of Lystra, he was the son of a Greek father and a Jewish mother (Acts 16:1). In his early youth he was influenced by the godly lives of his grandmother, Lois and his mother, Eunice (II Tim. 1:5; 3:15). He apparently was converted to Christ by Paul during the latter's first missionary journey (I Tim. 1:2, 18; cf. Acts 14:6–23).[2] Because of his spiritual gifts and Christian maturity, he was selected by Paul during the latter's second journey to become an associate in the missionary enterprise (Acts 16:1–3). At that time he

---

[1]Two early church fathers, Jerome and Augustine, both believed that Paul took his new name from Sergius Paulus.

[2]Paul's constant mention of Timothy as his son doubtless refers to the latter's conversion as well as to the close relationship which developed between them.

was circumcised and ordained (Acts 16:3; I Tim. 4:14; II Tim. 4:5).[3]

Timothy shared in the establishment of the work at Philippi, Thessalonica, and Berea (Acts 16:1–17:14). When he rejoined Paul at Athens, he was sent back to Thessalonica to continue the edification of that church (Acts 17:14–16; cf. I Thess. 3:1–2). He later returned to Corinth and assisted the apostle in the founding of that church (Acts 18:5).

The biblical record is silent as to whether Timothy traveled with Paul from Corinth to Ephesus to Caesarea to Jerusalem to Antioch and finally back to Ephesus (Acts 18:18–19:1). However, he did work with Paul at Ephesus (Acts 19:22). Paul then sent him into the provinces of Macedonia and Achaia to minister to the churches in those areas and to prepare the way for a proposed visit by Paul (Acts 19:22; cf. I Cor. 4:17; 6:10). Before Paul left Ephesus, Timothy rejoined him in that city (II Cor. 1:1, 19; Rom. 16:21).[4] He then traveled with Paul from Ephesus to Macedonia to Achaia back to Macedonia and on to the province of Asia (Acts 20:1–5).

Again, the biblical record is silent about the presence of Timothy with Paul on the latter's trip to Jerusalem, his arrest at the Holy City, his two-year imprisonment at Caesarea, and his voyage to Rome (Acts 21:1–28:16). He must have rejoined the apostle at Rome in the early months of the latter's imprisonment. From Rome he may have been sent to Philippi (2:19–24), although Paul's imminent release may have stopped that desire from being fulfilled.

After Paul's release, Timothy journeyed with Paul to Ephesus where he was left to care for the church (I Tim. 1:3). He was not with Paul when the latter was arrested and

[3]The circumcision of Timothy was not a contradiction of Paul's teaching (cf. Gal. 5:2–3). He was circumcised not to gain justification but to increase his effectiveness as a witness to Jewish audiences who knew his racial background (cf. I Cor. 9:19–20).

[4]Timothy was gone when Paul wrote I Corinthians, but he was with the apostle when II Corinthians was written. Note the respective omission and inclusion of his name in the salutations.

quickly taken to Rome; however, the apostle requested that he come (II Tim. 4:9). It is difficult to say whether Timothy did go to Rome and whether he arrived before the apostle's martyrdom. If Paul wrote the Letter to the Hebrews, there is some speculation that Timothy went to Rome, was imprisoned, and was later released (Heb. 13:23–24).[5] Tradition states that Timothy was martyred during the reign of either Domitian or Nerva.

Timothy, therefore, was well known to the Philippians. He had been in that city on at least three occasions and was prepared to go again (2:19–23). He was not only Paul's associate but he may have been the amanuensis who actually wrote the letter under the apostle's dictation and supervision.[6] At the same time, it cannot be said that he was a co-author of the contents. The epistle contains too many personal references to Paul to justify that conclusion. Since Paul and Timothy were like-minded, (2:20), the epistle did reflect the convictions and the feelings of the young associate.

3. *The position of Paul and Timothy*

Both men were "servants of Jesus Christ".[7] They were literally Christ's slaves *(douloi)*, bought and owned by Him. This is the only epistle where Paul uses such a descriptive word in apposition and applies it to both himself and his associate. Later, Paul wrote of Timothy "that, as a son with the father, he hath served with me in the gospel" (2:22). The verb "served" *(edouleusen)* means "to serve as a slave" and is related to the typical word for slave *(doulos)*. In ancient cultures, the sons born to slaves were automatically slaves themselves. In like fashion, Timothy was Paul's spiritual son and thus inherited his slavehood status and motivation from the apostle.

[5]The speculation could stand even if Hebrews were written by one other than Paul after the martyrdom of the apostle.

[6]Paul used secretaries in the composition of his other letters (Rom. 16:22; Gal. 6:11; II Thess. 3:17).

[7]The noun appears without the definite article. They were servants, but not the only servants of Christ.

In other epistles where the two names are mentioned together, the expressed relationships are different. Twice Paul called himself an apostle and named Timothy as his brother (II Cor. 1:1; Col. 1:1). Once he identified himself as a prisoner of Jesus Christ and his young associate as his brother (Philem. 1). Twice, he simply gave the names of three missionary team members without any further descriptions (I Thess. 1:1; II Thess. 1:1).

Normally, Paul designated himself as an apostle (I Cor. 1:1; Gal. 1:1; I Tim. 1:1; II Tim. 1:1). Twice he saw himself as both a servant and an apostle (Rom. 1:1; Titus 1:1). In both of these latter references, he knew that he was a servant first, then an apostle.[8]

To Paul and to the spiritually minded, the term *servant* was a title of dignity and humility. There was no greater position than to be the servant of Jehovah God. Moses was a servant (Exod. 14:31) and so were the prophets (Amos 3:7). Christ called the aged apostle John His servant (Rev. 1:1). There is no conflict between being the servant of God and the servant "of Jesus Christ," because Jesus Christ is God. Worship and service must always be joined and directed toward God only (cf. Matt. 4:10). Elsewhere, Paul exclaimed: "For we preach not ourselves, but Christ Jesus the Lord; and ourselves your servants for Jesus' sake" (II Cor. 4:5).

This positional title is appropriate to the tenor of the epistle. Service is one of the dominant themes because it is the outward manifestation of inner humility. At His incarnation, Christ took "the form of a servant" even though He was the sovereign Son of God (2:7). Paul, Timothy, and Epaphroditus all revealed the attitude of servility in their ministries (2:22, 25). The Philippians likewise needed to develop this Christlike attribute (2:3–5).

B. Readers (1:1b)

When Paul wrote to a local congregation, he addressed it in various ways. The Romans were beloved of God and saints

---

[8]Note the word order.

(Rom. 1:7). The Corinthians were the church of God, sanctified positionally, and called saints (I Cor. 1:1; II Cor. 1:1). Both the Ephesians and the Colossians were seen as the saints and the faithful (Eph. 1:1; Col. 1:2). The Thessalonians were the church located in God the Father and in God the Son (I Thess. 1:1; II Thess. 1:1). In all of these epistles, Paul viewed the local church in its corporate spiritual unity.

In this letter, however, he discriminated by dividing the membership into three categories. Within the family of God, there is a definite diversity within unity (Eph. 4:4–13). Thus, this epistle was written not just to the entire church, but also to individual groups within the assembly.

1. The saints

His first address is "to all the saints in Christ Jesus." The title "saints" (tois hagiois) is descriptive of all genuine believers. It is not restricted to an elite group of extremely spiritual persons nor does it refer to a few who are declared to be saints years after their deaths. These saints were living and were lay members of the church at Philippi.

The term saints literally means "set apart ones." It is based upon a verb (hagiazō) which means "to set apart" or "to sanctify." All believers have been set apart by God from the world at the time of their conversion and continue to remain in that sanctified position throughout their lives.[9] A distinction must be made between being a saint and being saintly. The former refers to a believer's position whereas the latter points to his practice. All believers are saints, but not all of them are saintly; however, they should endeavor to put their sanctified position into practice.

Nowhere in Scripture is any person by proper name ad-

[9]The word "sanctify" applies to four different stages of the believer's salvation. It refers to the ministry of the Holy Spirit in the person's life before conversion (Gal. 1:15; II Thess. 2:13); the time of regeneration (I Cor. 1:2, 6:11; Heb. 10:14); the present cleansing and edifying ministry of the Christian by the Spirit through the Word of God (John 17:17); and the total separation from the effects of sin when the believer receives the incorruptible, immortal body (Eph. 5:26–27).

dressed as "saint." The word normally appears in the plural and is used collectively of the entire family of God. In his closing remarks, Paul did employ the singular: "Salute every saint in Christ Jesus" (4:21). Even in this usage, however, the entire group is included.

The adjective "all" further reinforces the concept that no believer in Philippi is omitted from the address. Paul wrote to all (1:1); he prayed for all (1:4); he thought of all (1:7); he shared the grace of God with all (1:7); he longed after all (1:8); he persisted for all (1:25); he rejoiced with all (2:17); and he extended his benediction to all (4:23).

Sainthood is only possible because of one's position "in Christ Jesus." This concept thoroughly permeates the epistles of Paul. This is a distinctive sphere for the believer of this church age. A person gets *into* Christ and thus is *in* Christ by the baptism in the Holy Spirit, a ministry which first occurred on the day of Pentecost (Acts 1:5; I Cor. 12:13). When a believing sinner is "in Christ, he is a new creature; old things are passed away; behold, all things are become new" (II Cor. 5:17). He was once a condemned sinner in the world, but now he is an accepted child of God in Christ. His spiritual standing has been completely and permanently changed.

These opening remarks are contrary to human evaluations. Contemporary man would see the apostles as saints and the church members as servants; but here the apostle is a servant writing to the saints. This approach further marks the joy of humility which is emphasized throughout the letter.

2. The bishops

The "bishops" are the chief presiding officers of the local church. The term is based upon a compound Greek word (*episkopos*) which means "oversight" (*epi*, "over" and *skopos*, "sight").[10] It is derived from a verb (*episkeptomai*) which translates to "look upon" or "after," to inspect as an

---

[10]The denominational title *Episcopalian* is based upon this word.

overseer or a superintendent, comparable to the modern "foreman."

In a nontechnical sense, the title is applied to Jesus Christ, who is "the Shepherd and Bishop of your souls" (I Peter 2:25). Christ has the oversight over the universal church as its living head (Eph. 1:22–23), just as the bishop has oversight over a local church. The term was also applied to the apostolic oversight which Judas forfeited by his unbelief and apostasy (Acts 1:20).

The technical sense, however, is found in this passage. It is one of three terms used to describe the position of the leading church officers. The other two are "elder" *(presbuteros)*[11] and "shepherd" or "pastor" *(poimēn)*. The fact that they are used interchangeably or synonymously of the same group is demonstrated in the following passages. After Paul summoned the Ephesian elders *(presbuterous)*, he said to them: "Take heed therefore unto yourselves, and to all the flock, over the which the Holy Spirit hath made you overseers [*episkopous*], to feed [*poimainein*] the church of God" (Acts 20:17, 28). Peter also made the same triple identification when he addressed the elders *(presbuterous):* "Feed [*poimanate*] the flock of God which is among you, taking oversight [*episkopountes*] thereof, not by constraint, but willingly; not for filthy lucre, but of a ready mind" (I Peter 5:1–2).

Although the three terms describe the same person, it is possible to isolate their distinctive emphases. *First,* the concept behind "pastor" is to shepherd and to feed. The main responsibility here is the supply of spiritual nourishment through biblical teaching. A pastor must be a teacher, first and foremost (Eph. 4:11; I Tim. 3:2).[12] Pastoral care has three goals, delineated by Jesus Christ Himself: to teach the immature or new Christians (John 21:15), to teach adult believ-

---

[11]The denominational title *Presbyterian* is based upon this word.

[12]The Ephesians passage indicates that he must be a pastor-teacher. These are not two different positions.

ers (John 21:17), and to guide all the flock (John 21:16).[13] *Second,* the essence of the "bishop" is to render oversight, to see that the work of the local church is done correctly by the members who have been trained by him. *Third,* the term "elder" refers to the individual's position and to his respect by others.

In the first century, the apostles and their authenticated representatives appointed elders to oversee those churches which were established by them (Acts 14:23; Titus 1:5). Christ assigned this prerogative to the apostles when He established them as the ones who were to lay the foundation of the church age (Eph. 2:20). With the passing of the Apostolic Age, the responsibility to select elders rested with the churches themselves. They had the benefit of apostolic precedent plus the guidance of the inspired Scriptures which set forth the requirements of the office (I Tim. 3:7; Titus 1:5–9). Since local churches are now "the pillar and ground of the truth" (I Tim. 3:15), its protectors and propagators, they alone must appoint their leaders.

In the second century, a distinction was made between a bishop and an elder, with the former being acknowledged as superior to the latter. There is no biblical support, however, for making such a division. In addition, there is no indication that a bishop had oversight over a group of churches.

The usage of the plural shows that one church could have more than one bishop-elder-pastor. Since one city might contain several house churches, it could indicate that each assembly had one bishop. All believers within one community constituted one church regardless of their respective meeting places. They were both organically and organizationally joined together. This situation does not prevail today because of the various denominational groupings.

The word "bishops" actually occurs without the definite article ("the"). This shows that there was no prescribed number of bishops or deacons within a local church. The

---

[13]This distinction is clear in the Greek text: *boske ta arnia mou* (21:15); *poimane ta probata mou* (21:16) and *boske ta probata mou* (21:17).

multiplicity of these positions depended on the church's individual needs and upon the availability of qualified men.

Only men were appointed to the position of bishop. The designated qualifications could only apply to men. No woman was to have administrative headship over the man in either the home or the church (I Cor. 11:2–16; I Tim. 2:11–15).

Because of the time and effort involved in their work, the bishops were to be supported financially by the church (I Tim. 5:17–18; I Peter 5:2). The amount was to be in direct proportion to their effort and success (I Tim. 5:17).

3. The deacons

The "deacons" *(diakonois)* are those officers selected by the church to assist the bishop-pastor-elders. They should relieve the pastors of lesser responsibilities so that the pastors might be able to devote more time and energy to prayer and to preaching (Acts 6:4). They probably originated out of a need created by the rapid numerical growth of the church at Jerusalem (Acts 6:1–7). At that time, some widows murmured because they were being neglected in the daily ministration *(diakonia;* Acts 6:1). In recognition of the problem, the apostles exclaimed:

> It is not reason that we should leave the word of God, and serve *[diakonein]* tables.
> Wherefore, brethren, look ye out among you seven men of honest report, full of the Holy Spirit and wisdom, whom we may appoint over this business (Acts 6:2–3).

Seven men were then selected. Although the title *deacon* was not ascribed to them, two related words found in the passage are descriptive of their responsibilities.

Their qualifications are extremely high (I Tim. 3:8–13; cf. Acts 6:3). When the apostolic era ended, the local churches had to use these guidelines to choose their deacons. Just as the first deacons relieved the apostles of mundane cares, so the church office of deacon emerged to relieve the pastor of those responsibilities which could be assumed by lay members.

The Greek word *diakonos* and its derivatives are used in a nontechnical sense for a general ministry. Angels ministered to Christ at His temptation (Matt. 4:11), and they also serve believers (Heb. 1:14). Women ministered by giving financial assistance to the apostolic group (Mark 15:41). Preparing dinner was a ministry (Matt. 8:15). Christ ministered by giving His life on the cross (Matt. 20:28). Phoebe was a female servant, a deaconess of the church at Cenchrea (Rom. 16:1). It is debatable whether she had an official church position or that she simply served in a general sense. Some have suggested that the wives of the deacons served as deaconesses (cf. I Tim. 3:11). Paul regarded himself and Apollos as ministers of the Word (I Cor. 3:5).

The derivation of the word *deacon* is interesting. It is a compound word, based upon *dia* ("through") and *konis* ("dust"). The imagery suggests a man who quickly moves to perform his tasks and who kicks up a trail of dust by his haste. Deacons, therefore, must be dependable servants of the church and faithful assistants to the pastor.

II. THE BLESSING (1:2)

The typical Greek greeting employed the third person, but Paul conveyed a greater degree of intimacy by using the second person ("to you").

A. Its Content

The content of the blessing was twofold: "grace" and "peace." The first word reflects a Greek concept ("grace," *charis*), whereas the second manifests a Hebrew approach ("peace," *shalom*). Grace always precedes peace and forms the foundation for the latter.

1. Grace

All believers are saved or "justified freely by the grace of

God through the redemption that is in Christ Jesus" (Rom. 3:24). Their acceptable standing is maintained by divine grace (Eph. 2:8–9). The doctrine of grace reveals that God bestows blessings upon believing sinners apart from any merit within them. In addition, God supplies daily grace to meet the needs of the Christian, giving undeserved provision (John 1:16) and forgiving daily sins (Rom. 5:20). This apostolic blessing stresses daily grace. Although Paul constantly glorified the grace of God in his life and ministry, the word occurs only three times in this epistle (1:2, 7; 4:23).

2. Peace

When a sinner becomes a believing Christian, he gains an unalterable standing of peace with God or before God (Rom. 5:1). In the world, however, he needs the peace of God for daily protection from hostile pressures upon his mind and heart. Paul began and ended the epistle with a request for this sustaining peace (1:2; cf. 4:7, 9). If a believer could only see that each day of his life begins and ends with God's grace and peace, then he would have joy and stability. Leon Morris stated that peace is "not simply the absence of strife, but the presence of positive blessings. It is the prosperity of the whole man, especially his spiritual prosperity."[14] The word *peace* likewise appears three times in this epistle (1:2; 4:7, 9).

B. Its Source

The source of this blessing is from two persons within the divine being: "God the Father" and "the Lord Jesus Christ." One preposition, "from" *(apo)*, links the Father and the Son together as the common source.[15] Doubtless these gifts are mediated to the believer through the indwelling ministry of the Holy Spirit. One aspect of the fruit of the Spirit is peace (Gal. 5:22).

[14]Leon Morris, *The First Epistle of Paul to the Corinthians*, p. 35.

[15]The deity of Jesus Christ is affirmed in this verse by the divine title *Lord* (2:11; I Cor. 8:6) and by His union with the Father as the common source of grace and peace.

STAND UNITED IN JOY

Questions for Discussion

1. Do any men approximate the life and ministry of Paul today? Is it possible to do today what he did in the first century? Why, or why not?

2. How can modern Timothys be produced today? What should be the role of local churches in such development? Of seminaries? Of internships?

3. Do modern preachers see themselves as servants? Why, or why not?

4. What kind of service should churches expect of their pastors? Should printed job descriptions be given to pulpit candidates?

5. What types of church government are permitted within the teaching of Scripture? What types are prohibited?

6. To what extent should pastors get involved in the lives of church members? How often should they visit in the homes? Are most churches too large today in order to have proper pastoral care?

7. What areas of responsibility belong to the deacons? Should deacons be elected to short terms or to lifelong duties?

2

The Prayer from Prison
Philippians 1:3–11

The apprehension of the Philippians over the welfare of Paul was natural, but they had forgotten what kind of man the apostle really was. He never permitted adverse circumstances to control his destiny or to rob him of his present joy in the Lord. Whatever happened to him occurred for the furtherance of the gospel, not for its hindrance. His Roman imprisonment gave him time to write four inspired epistles: Ephesians, Philippians, Colossians, and Philemon. This ministry of correspondence justified the years spent under government arrest.

In addition, however, Paul had a ministry of prayer. During his two years of house internment (Acts 28:30), he had ample time to reflect, to remember, and to pray. The Philippians should have known that the apostle would be engaged in this spiritual activity. Their own church started as a result of similar circumstances. Shortly after Paul evangelized the Macedonian city, he and Silas were beaten and imprisoned for exorcising a demon out of a possessed girl (Acts 16:22–23). They were fastened in the stocks within the inner prison; but how did they respond? The Book of Acts states: "And at midnight Paul and Silas *prayed,* and *sang praises* unto God: and the prisoners heard them" (Acts 16:25). Prayers and praises! Instead of sobbing there was singing, and in place of pouting there was praying. They knew that they were in the will of God within that dungeon and thus they knew that God was working out all things for their good and His glory. The prisoners and the jailor heard those joyful anthems, and presumably, many of them believed in Christ as a result.

The prayers of Paul from prison produced salvation, an earthquake, and his subsequent release. At Rome the situation was no different. The apostle wanted his readers to know that he could pray in Rome and that his requests could be administered by God in Philippi and in all other cities throughout the empire.

I. HIS HEART TOWARD THEM (1:3-8)

Paul was not full of self-pity over his predicament; rather, he was concerned over the Philippians. Each verse in this section of six verses contains the mention of "you." There is "remembrance of you" (1:3), "prayer of mine for you all" (1:4), "your fellowship" (1:5), "good work in you" (1:6), "think this of you all" (1:7), "I have you in my heart" (1:7), "ye are all partakers" (1:7), and "I long after you all" (1:8). In his most dire need, he was benevolent, altruistic, and other-centered. He was thankful for their prayers, but more than anything he desired to pray for them. Paul was a giver by nature, not a receiver.

A. He Thanked God for Them (1:3)

All of the epistles written to churches, with the exception of Galatians and II Corinthians, begin with a prayer of thanksgiving (Rom. 1:8; I Cor. 1:4; Eph. 1:16; Phil. 1:3; Col. 1:3; I Thess. 1:2; II Thess. 1:3). All of the letters written to individuals, with the exception of Titus, likewise start in the same way (I Tim. 1:12; II Tim. 1:3; Philem. 4). The cause of this thanksgiving was what God had done for them and what He was presently doing through them. Included among the specific areas of special praise were a witnessing faith (Rom. 1:8), the grace of God and spiritual enrichment (I Cor. 1:4-5), saving faith and brotherly love (Eph. 1:15), hope of heaven (Col. 1:5), work of faith, labor of love, and patience of hope

(I Thess. 1:3; II Thess. 1:3–4). The Philippians undoubtedly possessed these qualities, but they would be praised specifically for their fellowship in the gospel (1:5).

Four features can be stated about this thanksgiving.

1. It was personal

Although Paul did not use the emphatic Greek first person personal pronoun *I (egō)*, he did employ a first personal singular verb. Timothy was included in the initial greeting but the thanksgiving was exclusively Pauline. He wrote: "I thank" (1:3), not "we thank."

In addition, the address of gratitude was to "my God." God was not distant or impersonal to the apostle; rather, He was a living person who was directly and intimately involved in Paul's affairs. During the troubled voyage to Rome, he could confidently assert to the frightened mariners and soldiers: "For there stood by me this night the angel of God, whose I am, and whom I serve" (Acts 27:23).

Paul's usage of this phrase should not be confused with the distinctive interpretation which Jesus Christ attached to those words. He told Mary Magdalene after His resurrection: "Go to my brethren, and say unto them, I ascend unto my Father, and your Father, and to my God, and your God" (John 20:17). God was the God and Father of the Lord Jesus Christ in a sense altogether different from the way in which He is the God and Father of believing sinners. The relationship between the Father and the Son is an infinite and eternal one within the divine being, whereas He is the God over His created world and the Father of His redeemed children. Paul willingly confessed the sovereign government of God over his entire life.

2. It was constant

The verb "thank" *(eucharistō)* denotes continuous action in present time.[1] Paul gave thanks for the Philippian believers

[1]It is present active indicative. A title for the ordinance of the Lord's Supper, *Eucharist,* is based upon a transliteration of this word (cf. I Cor. 11:24).

repeatedly, not just once. The verb is a compound word, based upon two ideas: *good* or *well (eu)* and *grace (charis)*. When the goodness of divine grace is perceived by the human soul, he will instinctively respond with grateful thanksgiving.

3. It was addressed to God

In ancient letters unearthed by archaeologists, the Romans and the Greeks began by giving thanks to their pagan gods. Here, Paul directed his praise to the one and only God of the universe, who also happened to be his God. The phrase literally reads: "to the God of me" *(tōi theōi mou)*. The usage of the definite article points out God's uniqueness. Elsewhere, the apostle wrote: "For though there be that are called gods, whether in heaven or in earth, (as there be gods many, and lords many,) But to us there is but one God, the Father, of whom are all things, and we by him" (I Cor. 8:5–6).

4. It was based upon remembrance

The preposition "upon" *(epi)* shows that the thanksgiving rested upon and was supported by memories. The following phrase ("every remembrance of you") has two alternative possibilities. It could mean that he thanked God because they remembered him in his afflication by their prayers and gifts, or it could be interpreted that he gave thanks everytime he remembered them.[2] Both concepts, of course, are true. When Paul thought of them, he considered what God had done in their midst and what they had done for him over the years in their unsolicited financial support (cf. 4:15). Both would provide sufficient grounds for thanksgiving.

B. He Made Request for Them (1:4–5)

It is possible to be thankful for someone without ever praying for that person. This perspective marks the behavior

---

[2]The first idea is based upon the view that the pronoun "you" is a subjective genitive, whereas the second position considers the pronoun to be an objective genitive.

of the unsaved person, but the outlook of Paul was altogether different. When he remembered a fellow believer, he thanked God for him.

1. The circumstances of the request (1:4)

The words "prayer" and "request" are two translations of the same Greek word *(deēsis)*. It refers to an entreaty or a supplication. Hendriksen states that it is a "petition for the fulfillment of a definite need that is keenly felt."[3] Later, the apostle does use the general word for prayer (1:9, *proseuchomai*). These requests of need can go from man to man as well as man to God; however, ordinary prayer *(proseuchē)* is limited from man to God only. In this passage, the request of Paul for the Philippians is directed toward God.

Five features about the request are given. *First,* it occurred during the apostle's devotional period ("in every prayer of mine"). Whenever requests were stated, he made supplication for the spiritual and financial needs of the church (4:19).[4] The adjective ("every") shows that the request was made often.

Second, the adverb ("always") indicates that he made a request whenever he remembered the Philippians. They were not always on his mind, but when they were, he always made an entreaty for them.

Third, he prayed for all of them ("for you all"). This included the bishops, the deacons, and all the saints (1:1). He was no respecter of titles. He did not divide that local manifestation of the body of Christ.

Fourth, he made requests continually. The verb "making" *(poioumenos)* points out constant activity and duration.[5] The earlier adverb ("always") reinforces that idea. Needs never

---

[3]William Hendriksen, *New Testament Commentary: Exposition of Philippians,* p. 51.

[4]The words "of mine" translate the subjective genitive *mou*. Paul was the subject of the verbal action of prayer. He prayed, not that he prayed for himself or that they prayed for him.

[5]It is a present middle participle.

go away, and neither should the supplications for those wants.

Fifth, the requests were made "with joy." Here is the first mention of this key word which marks the main theme of the epistle. When needs arise, the child of God should not manifest depression but show complete exhilaration. This is possible because he can make supplication to a God who knows, cares, and provides.

2. The basis of the request (1:5)

The foundation of the request was "fellowship." The word "for" is not a connective, but a preposition *(epi)* normally translated "upon"; thus, the fellowship supported the request. There can be no joyful supplications resting upon a faulty relationship. Three integral features are set forth.

First, the noun "fellowship" *(koinōnia)* denotes sharing, holding something in common. Biblical fellowship involves believers with one another and believers with God (I John 1:3). It is impossible for light to have "communion" (same word: *koinōnia)* with darkness (II Cor. 6:14); thus, Christians cannot have genuine fellowship with the unsaved.

Paul and the Philippians experienced a fellowship in the gospel (1:5), in grace (1:7), in the Holy Spirit (2:1), in the sufferings of Christ (3:10), and in giving (4:14–15). The mere bodily presence of two believers in the same activity does not constitute fellowship. True communion must advance the cause of Christ and stimulate the spiritual growth of believers. In fact, two Christians do not have to be together geographically in order to have fellowship. Paul and the Philippians were miles apart, yet they experienced it.

Second, their fellowship centered "in the gospel." The preposition "in" is really "into" *(eis).* Their fellowship actually advanced the gospel and was done in its interest. The Philippians prayed for Paul, gave to him, and witnessed to their own city. The "gospel" is clearly defined (cf. I Cor. 15:1):

> For I delivered into you first of all that which I also re-
> ceived, how that Christ died for our sins according to the
> scriptures;
> And that he was buried, and that he rose again the third day
> according to the scriptures (I Cor. 15:3–4).

Throughout the Scriptures, the gospel is described in several complementary ways. Its *source* is seen as the gospel of God (Rom. 1:1), its *savior* in the gospel of Christ (Rom. 1:16), its *standard* in the gospel of grace (Acts 20:24), its *substance* in the gospel of salvation (Eph. 1:13), and its *standing* in the gospel of peace (Eph. 6:15).

Third, their fellowship was constant ("from the first day until now"). It began at the time of their conversion under his ministry and it persisted until its present manifestation through the sending of Epaphroditus and a gift of money (4:18). Actually, the financial support of God's servants seems to have been at the forefront of this fellowship (cf. II Cor. 8:4; 9:13). They shared their substance with Paul when he labored in Thessalonica (4:14–16), and they did the same during his imprisonment at Rome.

C. He Had Confidence about Them (1:6)

Solomon wisely observed: "Confidence in an unfaithful man in time of trouble is like a broken tooth, and a foot out of joint" (Prov. 25:19). Man can disappoint, but God never fails. Paul did not place his confidence in the church per se; rather, it rested in God who had saved them and who was working out His sovereign purpose in and through them. He knew that God always finishes that which He has started. The verb "being confident" actually refers to a settled persuasion of mind and will which was the continuing result of a crisis decision in the past.[6] He knew what God had done and

---

[6]It is a perfect active participle *(pepoithōs)*. The perfect tense emphasizes a present state as a result of a past event.

was doing in his life, and he also knew that God would do the same in their lives.

1. God began a work in them

The nature of the confidence is indicated by the explanatory connective "that" *(hoti)*. It is further described in answers supplied to three implied rhetorical questions: Who did it? What was done? Where was it done?

First, God did the work. The verbal construction ("he which hath begun") points to God's personal involvement in their lives. It started in His eternal choice of them to salvation (Eph. 1:4), but in this passage, the emphasis is on the time of their conversion when God began to work in them.[7]

Second, the "good work" refers to the applied benefits of salvation secured by the gracious provision of Christ's substitutionary atonement. It includes a righteous standing before God (justification), a progressive deliverance from the power of the sin nature (sanctification), and the prospect of an immortal, incorruptible body (glorification). It is "good" *(agathon)* in that it corresponds to the very nature of God who alone is good in and of Himself (Mark 10:18; Rom. 3:12). A man becomes a Christian because God has begun to do a good work in him, not because he is doing good works for God (Eph. 2:8–10).

Third, the work was begun in them ("in you"). The preposition "in" *(en)*, which locates the sphere of operation, occurs twice, preceding the pronoun "you" and also being prefixed to the verb "begun" *(enarxamenos)*. This usage shows the personal, subjective acceptance of Christ's historical death and the convicting, regenerating work of the Holy Spirit. Later, Paul wrote: "Work out your own salvation.... For it is God which worketh in you both to will and to do of his good pleasure" (2:12–13). Genuine salvation involves a human response to a divine beginning.

[7]This conclusion is further supported by the fact that the verb is an aorist participle *(enarxamenos)*.

2. God will finish the work in them.

The apostle confessed elsewhere: "Faithful is he that call-eth you, who also will do it" (I Thess. 5:24). Here, two more features of his confidence are expressed. *First*, the certainty of completion is seen in the verb "will perform" *(epitelesei).*[8] God will thoroughly bring to a purposeful end any work which He has chosen to do. None can stay His hand.

Second, the time of completion is the "day of Jesus Christ." This phrase points to the coming of Christ to take believers unto himself. At that day it will involve resurrection for the Christian dead and translation for the living saved (I Cor. 15:51–53; I Thess. 4:16–17). According to God's sovereign purpose, believers are already glorified in His sight (Rom. 8:30). Men observe what is presently happening, but God looks at His people as they will be when He has finished His work in them. It is a biblical axiom that God "calleth those things which be not as though they were" (Rom. 4:17).

D. He Had Them in His Heart (1:7)

A familiar axiom states: "Absence makes the heart grow fonder." Since Paul was often separated geographically from his beloved spiritual children, he frequently expressed his affection through public correspondence (I Cor. 5:3; II Cor. 7:3; Col. 2:5; I Thess. 2:17). He was always present in spirit, rejoicing and agonizing over what was taking place in their church.

1. They were in his thoughts

The mind can never be divorced from the heart. True loving concern must stem from both as an expression of the total person. In this letter to the Philippians, great emphasis is placed upon a holy mind and right thinking (1:7; 2:2, 5; 3:15, 16, 19; 4:2, 7, 8). The verb "to think" means more than just

[8]The word *telescope* is based upon this Greek term. The prefix *(epi)* intensifies this unconditional promise. The verb stem *(telesei)* points to the achievement of a stated goal.

a mental exercise; it conveys a sympathetic interest and concern. The adjective "meet" *(dikaion)* literally means "right" or "just." Thus, a person who has been justified by God should manifest practical righteousness by altruistic attitudes.

2. *They were in his actions*

Genuine love is reciprocal. Paul had them in his heart, and they had him in their hearts.[9] This heart possession was continuous, not sporadic.[10] This concern occurred in two places. *First,* it was in his "bonds" *(desmois).* In his home, under house arrest and chained to soldiers, Paul thought about the Philippians (Acts 28:20, 30).

Second, it was "in the defence and confirmation of the gospel." In the Roman court, he acted as a representative for all of the churches. He thought of them through what he said ("defence") and what he did ("confirmation"). The word "defence" *(apologia)* refers to a logical, legal presentation of the truth (Acts 22:1; I Peter 3:15). In Paul's evangelistic outreach, the gospel was confirmed by God through the performance of miracles and sign-gifts (Mark 16:20; I Cor. 1:6–7; Heb. 2:3–4); however, there is no biblical indication that the apostle performed supernatural works before Caesar. Rather, he fostered a gracious deportment before the authorities.

3. *They were in his grace*

Both Paul and the Philippians were "partakers" *(sugkoinōnōus)* of grace. The word literally means "common with" or "sharers with." Both had been saved by grace, and both were experiencing sustaining grace in the midst of their respective trials.

[9]The Greek construction allows for either idea in this verse. The articular infinitive *(to echein;* translated "have") is followed by two accusative pronouns: "me" *(me)* and "you" *(humas).* Either one could be the subject of the verbal action, and the other could serve as the direct object. The word position and the following prepositional phrase argue mainly for the former view.

[10]Indicated by the present tense.

E. He Longed for Them (1:8)

1. It was witnessed by God

Paul used a solemn oath to support his loving concern for the church ("For God is my record"). In his epistles, he often did this (Rom. 1:9; II Cor. 1:23; I Thess. 2:5, 10). The word "record" is normally translated as "witness" (*martus.*).[11] Paul knew his heart, and he also knew that God was aware of his inner feelings.

2. It was an intense desire

The four words ("how greatly I long") actually translates into just one Greek verb (*epipothō*). The preposition prefix (*epi*) intensifies this strong term of desire. It was used of the athlete who strained at the finish line to finish first. The object of this emotion was them, not their money ("you all"). He could honestly say to them: "I seek not yours, but you" (cf. II Cor. 12:14). Later, he identified the Philippians as "my brethren dearly beloved and longed for, my joy and crown" (4:1).

3. It reflected Christ

The sphere of desire was "in the bowels of Jesus Christ." The term "bowels" (*splagchnois*) refers to the viscera, the internal organs of the body, including the heart, liver, and intestines. Symbolically and spiritually, it came to mean the seat of emotions, with stress upon the feelings of love, compassion, and tenderness. The apostle's love for the Philippians manifested Christ's love for mankind and for the church. As Christ was compassionate, so was Paul. It was really Christ desiring them through him (cf. Gal. 2:20).

II. HIS PRAYER FOR THEM (1:9–11)

The fact of prayer was mentioned earlier (1:3–4); its content is now set forth ("and this I pray"). A believer must have

---

[11]Since it stands first in the Greek sentence, it is greatly emphasized.

an intense, loving concern for another before he can pray effectively. Five goals of this specific prayer are expressed.

A. Abounding Love (1:9)

When a sinner believes unto salvation, the love of God is shed in his heart by the initial infilling and the permanent indwelling of the Holy Spirit (Rom 5:5). He not only loves God, but he also loves the children of God in whom the same Savior abides (I John 4:19). He is taught by God to love his spiritual brothers (I Thess. 4:9), and this fact alone gives assurance of personal salvation (I John 3:14). This implanted seed of love, however, must grow. It must be cultivated and manifested daily. It must not be limited or contained.

1. Its abundance

The imagery behind this verse is that of a river overflowing its banks during a flood. Love is the river, and its two banks which form its channel and direction are "knowledge" and "judgment." Christian love must not be a stagnant pool or a slow moving trickle; rather, it must be a raging torrent.

According to the verb, love must constantly keep on overflowing ("may abound").[12] This concept is further reinforced by the descriptive adverbial phrase ("yet more and more"). A flooding river grows wider as more water flows into its system.

2. Its control

Love, however, must never be misdirected. Even a raging river is moving toward a destination within certain bounds. The two guidelines of genuine biblical love are now enumerated. *First,* it must be expressed in "knowledge" *(epignōsei).* This refers to a thorough, mental grasp of spiritual truth. He must "be filled with the knowledge of His will in all wisdom and spiritual understanding" (Col. 1:9). True love does

---

[12]Indicated by the present active subjunctive.

not act in ignorance. A believer must know *what* and *whom* to love.

Second, it must be in "judgment" *(aisthēsei).* True love must discriminate between good and evil (Heb. 5:14), between important and unimportant issues (I Cor. 3:13–23). A believer must know *how* to love. Such love must reveal spiritual perception of divine beauty and worth.

B. Discerning Approval (1:10a)

A believer must "approve things that are excellent." This action can only be the purpose or result of discerning love.[13] The verb "approve" was used for assaying metals. It means to test with the sense of approval. Each believer must internalize his conviction of what is right. In moral absolutes he must be committed to God's holy standards, but in ever-changing cultural situations he must critically examine his area of soul-liberty. The present tense of the verb indicates that a believer must constantly reassess his opinions and lifestyle.

The "excellent things" are actually "the things which differ" *(ta diapheronta).* The difference is not between good and evil, because God decrees that distinction. Rather, it is between the primary and the secondary, between eternal and temporal values. As situations of life change, so do the things which differ; thus this analysis must be maintained daily.[14]

C. Blameless Deportment (1:10b)

The connective "that" *(hina)* shows the third purpose of the prayer.

---

[13]The word "that" actually introduces a purpose or result of the preceding action. The construction consists of a preposition *(eis)* with an articular infinitive *(to dokimazein).*

[14]Indicated by the present participle.

STAND UNITED IN JOY

1. *Its description*

Two qualities are given. *First,* they should be "sincere." The word literally means to be "judged by the sun" *(eilikrineis).* Ancient jars and vases were examined for disguised cracks by holding them up against the rays of the sun. Hypocrites can fool man, but God knows their thoughts and intents (Heb. 4:12).

Second, they should be "without offence" *(aproskopoi).* They should not be like an uneven sidewalk against which a man could stub his toe and fall. He must give no offense "to the Jews, nor to the Gentiles, nor to the church of God" (I Cor. 10:32). A person offends when he lives selfishly.

2. *Its duration*

The active pursuit of this goal must last an entire lifetime or "till the day of Christ." This latter expression points to the coming of Christ and the subsequent judgment seat (1:6; II Cor. 5:10). If a Christian lives in the light of the imminent return, he will live a godly life (I John 3:1–3).

D. Righteous Character (1:11a)

1. *Its nature*

Righteous fruit can issue only from a righteous root. A believing sinner has a justified position before a holy God, but he has the personal responsibility to put that new standing into practice. John wrote: "he that doeth righteousness is righteous, even as he is righteous (I John 3:7; cf. 2:29).

Paul prayed that they might be permanently "filled with the fruits of righteousness."[15] These fruits (plural) doubtlessly include the fruit (singular) of the Spirit (Gal. 5:22–23), the fruit of soul-winning (Rom. 1:13), the fruit unto holiness (Rom. 6:22), the fruit of good works (Col. 1:10), and the fruit of thanksgiving (Heb. 13:15).

---

[15]The verb is a perfect passive participle *(peplērōmenoi)* and should be seen as a periophrastic used with "may be" (1:10).

2. *Its source*

These fruits are "by Jesus Christ." Jesus said to His disciples: "I am the vine, ye are the branches: He that abideth in me, and I in him, the same bringeth forth much fruit: for without me ye can do nothing" (John 15:5). A branch in and of itself cannot produce fruit; rather, it must allow the life of the vine to flow through it. In a like manner, the believer who wants to live His life through the Son of God must be yielded to the indwelling Christ (1:21; Gal 2:20). Thus, the "fruits of righteousness" are really equivalent to the life in Christ.

E. Glory of God (1:11b)

If the four previous goals of the prayer would be achieved, then the ultimate result would be "the glory and praise of God." The glory of God magnifies who He is, and the praise of God rejoices over what He has done. You cannot have one without the other. His attributes and His actions can never be separated.

Questions for Discussion

1. Why do Christians forget what other believers have done for them? For others? How can their memories be renewed?

2. Why are Christians not as thankful as they should be? Is there any solution?

3. What are the strengths of modern prayer meetings? What are their weaknesses?

4. In what areas of life should believers manifest confidence? Do Christians ever think that God has failed them? Why?

5. How can love be balanced by knowledge and judgment? Give some contemporary illustrations.

6. What steps should be followed in testing the things which differ? Are there objective criteria? Subjective?

7. Do Christians govern their behavior by a belief in Christ's return?

3

The Opportunities of Obstacles
Philippians 1:12–19

To the average person, the good life is a trouble-free life. He is most happy when there are no illnesses, no accidents, no house repairs, and no job layoffs. Unfortunately, many Christians feel the same way.

Jesus Christ said, however, that the godly life would involve tribulations (John 16:33). Paul likewise predicted: "Yea, and all that will live godly in Christ Jesus shall suffer persecution" (II Tim. 3:12). The presence of evil men and demonic spirits in a hostile world makes it impossible for a believer to be at ease on this planet. There are bound to be conflicts, and the child of God must realize that he is a member of a minority.

How should such opposition be viewed? How should it be received? At all times, a believer should return good for evil (Luke 6:27–29; Rom. 12:17–21). He should seek to turn the adversity into an opportunity to glorify God. He must approach all obstacles to his spiritual advancement with realism and optimism, not with pessimism. The Philippians needed to learn this lesson, and so do we today.

I. THE PRINCIPLE STATED (1:12)

The church at Philippi became upset when they heard about Paul's imprisonment at Rome. The believers felt sorry for him. They worried that his ministry had been seriously impaired and that he might possibly die as a martyr. They thought that Paul's age and weak physical condition were slowing down his effectiveness. To show their concern, the church sent one of their members, Epaphroditus, to make personal inquiry of Paul and to give him financial assistance (2:25; 4:10, 18).

A. Things Will Happen to a Believer (1:12a)

The direct address ("Brethren") is now first used to arrest their attention (cf. 2:12; 3:1, 13, 17; 4:1, 8). He desired them to understand a fundamental premise, and he wanted them to keep it in mind always ("But I would ye should understand").[1]

1. The meaning of things

The general phrase ("the things which happened unto me") literally means "the according to me things" *(ta kat eme).*[2] It would be a close equivalent to the modern phrase "my affairs." Although many of his friends accompanied him on his hazardous missionary journeys and were exposed to similar adverse circumstances, Paul did not include them directly in the expression of this principle.

2. The list of things

What had happened to Paul since he had last seen the Philippians? Although he did not itemize the obstacles in this letter, he did discuss them elsewhere (II Cor. 11:23–27). Luke recorded the historical background of that period of the apostle's life (Acts 20:6–28:31).

---

[1]The verb "ye should understand" is really a present active infinitive *(ginōskein).* The active voice indicates that they were to put themselves into the learning process. This verb is also emphasized, because it appears first in the sentence.

[2]Note that the words "which happened" appear in italics in the KJV.

STAND UNITED IN JOY

At the end of his third missionary journey, Paul determined to go to Jerusalem with a special welfare collection given by the Gentile churches to the Jewish believers (Rom. 15:25–26). He fully expected to visit Rome and Spain after this project was completed (Rom. 15:23–24). At the same time, he knew that trouble awaited him in Jerusalem:

> And now, behold, I go bound in the Spirit unto Jerusalem, not knowing the things that shall befall me there:
> Save that the Holy Spirit witnesseth in every city, saying that bonds and afflictions abide me (Acts 20:22–23).

Other Christians warned him not to go, but he felt constrained not to heed their counsel (Acts 21:4). Even the prophet Agabus predicted that Paul would be arrested and bound over to the Roman government authorities (Acts 21:10–11). At this late stage, the associates of the apostle, including Luke, tried to prevent him from going, but they were unsuccessful (Acts 21:12–14).[3]

At Jerusalem, he consented to the request of the church elders to purify himself at the temple as a testimony to the Jewish believers who were still zealous for the law. When unbelieving Jews sighted the apostle in the court of the Israelites, they began to beat him to death (Acts 21:22–31). The Roman soldiers rescued him and bound him with chains (Acts 21:33). When a conspiracy to murder Paul was discovered by the authorities, he was secretly taken to the Roman garrison at Caesarea (Acts 21:23). There he remained as a prisoner for two years (Acts 24:27).

Paul then appealed to have his case tried by Caesar in Rome; thus, he undertook a voyage surrounded by soldiers (Acts 25:10–12). He then encountered a storm, a shipwreck, and a desperate swim to safety (Acts 27:14–20, 41–44). After a short stay at Melita (Malta), he finally arrived in Rome, where

---

[3]In that passage, note the reference to the author of Acts in the pronoun "we."

he would spend the next two years under house arrest (Acts 28:16, 30–31).

By this time other churches were also concerned about the apostle, so he sent Tychicus to both Ephesus and Colosse in order that they too might know what happened to him (Eph. 6:21; Col. 4:7).[4]

B. Things Can Advance the Gospel (1:12b)

The abverb "rather" shows the contrast between the cause and the effect. To Paul, opportunity was on the other side of obstacle. When a believer views adverse circumstances from the divine perspective, he will use them for spiritual advantage. Most Christians, unfortunately, permit difficulties to affect their emotional and mental stability. The Psalmist expressed it well: "Surely the wrath of man shall praise thee: the remainder of wrath shalt thou restrain" (Ps. 76:10).

The positive result of adversity is stressed here ("unto the furtherance of the gospel"). The preposition ("unto" *eis*) indicates purpose, goal, or result. A believer must look at the result of the adversity, not at the adversity itself. The Israelites saw in the onrushing Egyptian chariots a sign of destruction, but Moses recognized that predicament to be an opportunity for divine salvation (Exod. 14:13).

The term "furtherance" *(prokopēn)* literally means "to cut toward." It was a military term, used of engineers who would prepare a road for the advancing army by removing obstructions such as rocks and trees. Paul did not view difficulty with self-pity. He was not concerned how circumstances affected him; rather, he asked the question: How can this problem be used to proclaim the gospel in a distinctive way? Paul saw a beginning in what some called an end, and he walked through open doors which others concluded to be closed and locked.

---

[4]In those two passages, the same Greek phrase occurs *(ta kat eme)*. In Ephesians, it is translated as "my affairs," and in Colossians it is seen as "my state."

In such manner, God programmed the hardships of Joseph unto the preservation of the covenant people (Gen. 45–48; 50:18–21). God changed the curse put upon the Jews by Haman into a blessing (Esther 7:1–10). In the greatest display of divine sovereignty, Peter exclaimed concerning Christ: "Him, being delivered by the determinate counsel and foreknowledge of God, ye have taken, and by wicked hands have crucified and slain" (Acts 2:23). In confidence, the believer must face obstacles with this confession: "And we know that all things work together for good to them that love God, to them who are the called according to his purpose" (Rom. 8:28).

The verb "have fallen out" also emphasizes the lasting effects of past difficulties.[5] It literally means "have come" (*eleluthen*).

II. THE ILLUSTRATIONS GIVEN (1:13–19)

At this point, Paul wanted to inform the Philippians how God had used his arrest and subsequent two imprisonments to advance the gospel message. These results are indicated by the connecting words "so that" (*hoste*).[6]

A. Personal Witness (1:13)

1. Its nature

Paul was no ordinary prisoner. This fact soon became evident to those authorities who were involved in his case. The opening words are literally translated: "So that my bonds manifest in Christ might become...." The prepositional phrase ("in Christ") actually follows the adjective ("manifest") rather than the noun ("bonds"). It was soon known that the apostle was before the Roman court because he was a Christian, not because he had committed a civil crime. Paul himself knew that he was there by the will of God. The gov-

---

[5] It is a perfect active indicative of *erchomai*.
[6] This Greek term always introduces a result clause.

ernment may have thought that he was its prisoner, but he recognized that he was really "the prisoner of the Lord" (Eph. 4:1). He was an "ambassador in bonds" (Eph. 6:20).

Thus, Paul was in Rome not as a defendant but as a witness. He asked his friends to pray for this unique opportunity of outreach.

> And for me, that utterance may be given unto me, that I may open my mouth boldly, to make known the mystery of the gospel,
>
> For which I am an ambassador in bonds: that therein I may speak boldly, as I ought to speak (Eph. 6:19–20; cf. Col. 4:3–4).

2. *Its location*

Two spheres of witness are mentioned. *First,* he spoke "in all the palace." The term "palace" *(praitŏriō)* is normally transliterated as "praetorium." As such, it can refer either to places or persons.

The term was used of "the hall of judgment" where Pilate tried Christ in Jerusalem (John 18:28). It was also used in referring to "Herod's judgment hall" in Caesarea where Paul gave one of his defenses (Acts 23:35). At Rome, it was the court of Caesar on Palatine Hill. Thus, the *praetorium* was a place, the legal residence of Roman government officials. Some have identified it as the camp or barracks of the crack imperial guard.

It is more likely, however, that in his use of this technical term Paul refers to the praetorium soldiers themselves.[7] There were originally nine or ten thousand of these hand-picked soldiers who served Caesar personally. They received double pay and special privileges. They soon became so powerful that the aspirants to the throne tried to solicit their support. Since Paul was chained constantly to a soldier during his two years of house arrest, he was able to witness to the guard. The guard also observed how Paul spoke to his

---

[7]The next phrase ("among all the rest") further supports this conclusion.

friends, how he wrote, and how he prayed. The guardsmen were changed every six hours; thus in two years, the apostle would have been able to witness to almost 3,000 soldiers.[8]

Second, he spoke "in all other places." Literally this means "in all the remaining ones" *(tois loipois pasi).* No doubt he had the opportunity to give witness to other types of soldiers, to household servants, and to the government officials, including Nero.

Was the witness successful? In the conclusion of the epistle, he wrote: "All the saints salute you, chiefly they that are of Caesar's household" (4:22). These people, who were servants and/or relatives of Nero, must have been saved through the apostle's personal testimony. The Philippians should have known that this could have happened because Paul had led the jailor of their city and his family to Christ (Acts 16:30–34).

B. Encouragement of Preachers (1:14–18)

Preachers and their families live in glass houses. Both church members and outsiders are watching them from all angles at all times. Paul knew that his life was under constant scrutiny by both friend and foe. He recognized that his deportment before the Roman authorities could be a means of encouragement or discouragement. He wanted to be an ideal example.

1. Many received boldness to speak (1:14)

The presence of Paul in Rome as a political prisoner caused a stir within the local church. A few became timid in their witness, but the majority were stimulated to intensify their evangelistic efforts among the pagan Romans. Four descriptions of this latter group are given.

First, they constituted the majority within the church. The term *many* is literally "the more parts" *(tous pleionas).*[9] The

[8]Assuming that no guard was stationed with Paul twice.

[9]It is a comparative adjective used with the sense of the superlative.

usage of the Greek definite article *(tous)* shows that Paul was referring to a specific group.

Second, they were definitely saved. Their relationship to the apostle is seen in the title "the brethren," and their standing before God is indicated by the prepositional phrase "in the Lord."

Third, they received inner confidence through his example. The phrase ("waxing confident by my bonds") shows that they were persuaded to make a decision to stand for the truth regardless of the consequences.[10] They manifested that private decision by a display of public testimony.

Fourth, they were "much more bold to speak the word without fear." It is very natural to fear what people will think or do when a person orally proclaims the Word of God. This reluctance, however, can be overcome. Jesus had to encourage His disciples: "And fear not them which kill the body, but are not able to kill the soul" (Matt. 10:28). Even Paul had to stir up his young associate Timothy: "For God hath not given us the spirit of fear; but of power, and of love, and of a sound mind. Be not thou therefore ashamed of the testimony of our Lord, nor of me his prisoner" (II Tim. 1:7–8). The infinitive "to speak" *(lalein)* shows that their bold proclamation continued throughout the apostle's imprisonment.[11]

2. *Some preached out of bad motivation (1:15a, 16)*

This majority group was divided into two groups, indicated by the double usage of "some" *(tines).* Both preached the same message of Christ's death and resurrection ("preach Christ"), but each party had different reasons for doing so.

The faulty motivation of the first group is characterized in six ways. *First,* they witnessed "even of envy and strife."[12] The word *of (dia)* is normally translated "because of" or "on

---

[10]The verb "waxing confident" *(pepoithotas)* is a perfect active participle, the same verb as in 1:6.

[11]It is a present active infinitive.

[12]This phrase is emphasized in the sentence, occurring first and before the verb.

account of"; thus, the cause of their preaching was at fault, not its content. Envy *(phthonon)* is a work of the flesh, a sin caused by a lack of yieldedness to the Holy Spirit and a lack of love to the brethren (Gal. 5:16, 21, 26; I Peter 2:1). It is an expression of the unsaved life, although Christians too are capable of committing it (Rom. 1:29; Titus 3:3). Paul warned about such teachers whose ministries produced this result (I Tim. 6:4). Pilate knew that the religious officials had delivered Jesus out of envy (Matt. 27:18). In other words, envy is jealousy. These men preached Christ because they were jealous of Paul's success and popularity.

Second, the result of envy is "strife" *(erin),* sometimes translated as "wrangling" or "contention." Envy is the inward emotion, whereas strife is the outward expression.[13] It is also a work of the flesh (Gal. 5:20), an expression of the unsaved life (Rom. 1:29, "debate"), and a result of false teaching (I Tim. 6:4). Believers should strive to avoid this sin (Rom. 13:13; Titus 3:9). Unfortunately, it was the main sin which caused the party divisions within the church at Corinth (I Cor. 1:11, "contentions"). Strife is caused when people argue over the way a person words his theological position: "He just doesn't say it the way I want him to say it." Strife results when Christians choose to follow certain leaders to the neglect of others (I Cor. 3:3). It is mere carnality when men respond to disagreement like unsaved persons.

Third, they preached out "of contention" *(eritheias).* The preposition "of" *(ex)* shows the source of their proclamation.[14] Contention and strife are related (based upon the same Greek stem), and yet different. Both appear together as two separate works of the flesh (Gal. 5:20; "variance" [eris] and "strife" [eritheias]). Contention places attention upon the cause of personal rivalry which is selfish ambition. Paul later discouraged this lack of humility (2:3).

Fourth, they did not preach "sincerely" *(hagnōs).* This ad-

---

[13]They are joined together as the double objects of the same preposition.

[14]There are two different Greek words used to translate "preach": *kērussousin* (1:15) and *kataggellousin* (1:16).

verb is related to the adjective which means "pure, chaste, undefiled, and guiltless" *(hagnos)*. It was used of that which was holy, and sacred—free from ceremonial defilement. These teachers had impure motivations. They preached not because they loved Christ, but because they loved their own reputations.

Fifth, they intended to aggravate Paul ("supposing to add affliction to my bonds"). They hoped that Paul would become jealous when he saw them increasing their following. It was a subtle attack upon the apostle's psychological stability. The word "affliction" *(thlipsin)* literally means "friction." It carries a vivid image of the painful rubbing of the iron chains against a prisoner's arms and legs.

Sixth, they spoke "in pretence" *(prophasei;* 1:18). This is pious hypocrisy. The Pharisees used it as a "cloak for their sin" (John 15:22). They made long prayers, but they devoured the houses of widows (Matt. 23:14). This is the term used of the fearful sailors who lowered the life boat for their own safety while pretending to be casting out the anchor (Acts 27:30).

3. *Some preached out of good motivation (1:15b, 17)*

The contrast between the two different groups of preacher is seen in the double connectives "indeed" and "an *(men . . . de).*[15] There is no indication in the passage as which group constituted the majority. It would seem that Roman church, to whom Paul wrote and which contain large group of his friends (Rom. 16), would have been sympathetic toward the apostle.

Four features of this group are enumerated. *First,* spoke because of "goodwill" *(eudokian)*. The word "that which seems to be good." It involves free choice termination which brings a holy pleasure to oneself benefit to the object of that choice. This group lo preach Christ, and they wanted to encourage Paul. T is used of the pleasure of God when He chose to rev

[15]They usually mean: "On the one hand . . . on the other."

to babes (Matt. 11:25–26), to predestinate men to sonship (Eph. 1:5), to disclose His redemptive purpose to believers (Eph. 1:9), and to work within the lives of Christians (2:13). Paul used it of his heart's desire for the salvation of Israel (Rom. 10:1).

Second, they preached out of "love" *(agapēs).* In this context, the love is directed basically toward Paul. They loved him for who he was, for what he did for others, and for what he had done for them. Love for the brethren, of course, always reflects love for Christ. They were constrained to preach by the love of Christ (II Cor. 5:14).

Third, they knew why Paul was in prison ("knowing that I am set for the defence of the gospel"). They knew that Paul was there as the representative of them and of the gospel itself (cf. 1:7). The trial of the apostle was really a defense of the gospel message of redemption through Christ. In that sense, it was a trial of Jesus Christ Himself. The "defence" *(apologian)* was a logical presentation of facts and arguments designed to show that Christianity was not opposed to the government of Rome or any racial group, but rather that it was a blessing for the total man of all races. The goal was to establish the legitimacy of the Christian faith as a recognized religion within the Roman empire. The verb "I am set" *(keimai)* is a military term, used of a soldier who was on duty as a guard. The apostle was a soldier of the cross, who protected the integrity of the gospel message in churches, synagogues, and prisons.

Fourth, they spoke "in truth." Their lives were transparent. Both the content and the motivation of their message was true. Truth is that which corresponds to the true character of God. No error could be found in what they said, how they spoke it, and why they preached.

4. All preached Christ (1:18)

In his analysis of the self-motivated preachers, Paul came to two conclusions. *First,* regardless of their motivation, the content of their message was orthodox. They did preach Christ (1:14, 15, 16, 18). Some have tried to identify this

group with the Judaizers, whom the apostle later condemned (3:1-2, 17-19). The Judaizers, however, preached a false gospel of salvation through legalistic works (II Cor. 11:13-15; Gal. 1:6-9). They preached another Christ, one whom Paul did not proclaim (II Cor. 11:4). There would be no way that he could have rejoiced over the erroneous content of the legalists. But this group, though wrongly motivated, was theologically correct in the doctrines of Christology and soteriology.

This passage also shows that to preach the Word of God is to preach Christ (1:14; cf. 1:15, 16, 18). The only Christ that can be proclaimed is the Christ of the Scriptures. The content of His person and work must be derived solely from a logical exposition of the inspired, written Word of God.

Second, Paul could rejoice over the proclamation of their message ("and I therein do rejoice, yea, and will rejoice"). He could not rejoice over their faulty motivation, but he could rejoice that their gospel was sound in content, that Christ was magnified, that sinners were regenerated, and that they themselves were saved brethren.

The opening words of the verse introduce Paul's verdict ("What then? not withstanding, every way"). In effect, he said: "Well, what of it?" The main impact of their jealous preaching was the increased outreach of the gospel; and to the apostle, getting the gospel out, regardless of means ("every way"), was the most important goal in his life.

C. Increase of Support (1:19)

It was conceivable that the apostle could be found guilty and that he be martyred as a Roman criminal (1:20-21); however, he fully expected to be set free (1:24-25). He later expressed his hope to see the Philippians again (2:24-25). He even asked Philemon to prepare the guest room for him (Philem. 22). His conviction about his forthcoming release is here stated in the verb "I know" *(oida),* an inner persuasion conveyed by the indwelling Spirit. The fact of release is seen in the phrase "my salvation." This expression does not refer to spiritual salvation, which he already possessed, but to deliverance from his lengthy period of custody under the Romans. The dilemma of his imprisonment was finally coming to a climax, and he fully expected to be vindicated.

Such things as a release from prison do not happen on their own. Paul knew that, and he predicated his freedom upon two means of support.

1. By man

One means of support was the intercession of believers ("through your prayer"). Some have questioned why they should pray if God already has determined what He will do. These people fail to recognize that God has also chosen to work through human instrumentality. The release of Peter from Herod's dungeon was accomplished through the faithful prayers of the local church (Acts 12:12). Mordecai knew that God would deliver the Jewish people from the plot of Haman, but he also knew that Esther's elevation to queen might be the divine means to be employed (Esther 4:13-14).

The word "prayer" *(deēseōs)* refers to intense intercession, the same ministry that Paul was conducting in their behalf (1:4). When believers lovingly pray for each other, then God will accomplish His work. He works in and through man, not apart from him. Paul thus wrote to Philemon: "... for I trust that through your prayers I shall be given unto you" (Philem. 22).

2. By God

In the program of redemption, God and man are colaborers (I Cor. 3:9). The prayers of saints and the provision of God are two complementary sides of the same divine-human activity.

Divine help is here called "the supply of the Spirit of Jesus Christ." The word "supply" *(epichorēgias)* is a double compound word *(epi, choros,* and *hēgeomai)* which means "to furnish supplies for a musical chorus." In ancient times, a benefactor would pay for the singers and the dancers at a festival. In time, the word came to mean "to provide generously." In medical terminology, it was used of the joints and ligaments which joined two bones together (Eph. 4:16). The imagery is very clear. Paul and the Philippians, two members of the body of Christ, were joined together by prayer and the omnipresent, indwelling ministry of the Holy Spirit in spite of geographical distance.

The Spirit is called "the Spirit of Jesus Christ" because he was sent by the Son as well as by the Father and because He glorified Christ at all times (John 15:26; 16:14).

Questions for Discussion

1. What specific adversities can happen to a believer? Can he ever be prepared to meet such adversity?

2. How can the gospel be furthered by adversity? By death? By illness? By accident?

3. Why do Christians suffer depression? What can be done to gain victory over self-pity and frustration?

4. How can Christians encourage other believers? In what ways do they sometimes discourage them?

5. In what ways can a person with a faulty motivation proclaim truth? Should we cooperate with such individuals?

6. Should Baptists rejoice over the successes of Presbyterians? Methodists over that of Pentecostals? In what areas do denominational distinctions disrupt mutual rejoicing?

7. Why should believers pray for one another? How can it be encouraged? Why do not more attend the prayer service?

4

The Blessings of Life and Death
Philippians 1:20–26

People naturally rejoice at births, but they mourn at funerals. After all, a birth is the beginning of life, whereas a death is the end of life. To most, death is a dark shadow, the grim reaper, the unwelcome guest.

Paul, however, did not share this perspective on life and death. To him, death was the bridge between two distinctive expressions of life. It was the end of an old life, but it was also the beginning of a new and glorious life. Thus he could rejoice in either circumstance and could use both for the glorification of God.

The Philippians wanted the apostle to live, but they were afraid that he would soon die as a martyr. For them, only Paul's living would bring advantages; however, this outlook reflected a subtle selfishness. They needed to look at the apostle's life and death options through his eyes and from the divine perspective.

I. FOR PAUL (1:20–24)

In these four verses there is no mention given to the church (e.g., "you"); rather, the apostle is giving his analysis of his imprisonment, the possibility of death, and the likelihood of release.

THE BLESSINGS OF LIFE AND DEATH

A. His Testimony (1:20)

This verse contains two main verbal concepts, introduced by a qualifying prepositional phrase. Through this grammatical structure, Paul included three ideas within his testimony.

1. He had hope.

The opening preposition "according to" *(kata)* shows the standard behind Paul's confession. There is one object of that preposition with a double feature ("my earnest expectation and my hope").[1] *Expectation* is the outward manifestation of hope, whereas *hope* is the inward conviction of heart. The former is the effect, and the latter is the cause.

The noun "expectation" *(apokaradokian)* is unique. It is a double compound word, made up of *apo* ("from"), *kara* ("head"), and *dokeō* ("to be of opinion, suppose, or think"). In ancient times it was used of the spectator who sat on the edge of his seat and stretched his neck to see the outcome of an athletic event. Thus it meant to watch anxiously, with strained expectancy and eager longing. Elsewhere it is used of the animal creation which anticipates a deliverance from the curse when the children of God receive their new bodies (Rom 8:19).

The word "hope" *(elpida)* denotes one of the three main Christian virtues (I Cor. 13:13). It refers to a settled assurance of heart caused by a firm conviction that what is believed will come to pass. Of it, Paul wrote:

> For we are saved by hope: but hope that is seen is not hope: for what a man seeth, why doth he yet hope for?
>
> But if we hope for that we see not, then do we with patience wait for it (Rom. 8:24–25).

---

[1] The *Granville Sharp rule* is expressed here. It states that when two nouns joined by *and* are introduced by a single definite article, they are two descriptions of the same thing. The Greek construction is *tēn apokaradokian kai elpida mou.*

All committed believers are looking for the "blessed hope," namely, the coming of Jesus Christ (Titus 2:13). Thus, hope is not a crossing of the fingers, a naive wishful thinking against great odds; rather, it is a divinely implanted response to the sure promises of God.

Consequently, Paul had an expectant hope that he would be released, that he would see the Philippians again (1:25–26), that he would live to have further service, and that he would see Christ, either at his death or at His coming. The apprehension of the Philippians needed to be replaced by the anticipation of Paul.

2. He was not ashamed

Shame should not become a blot upon the family of God which bears His name. God is not ashamed to be called their God (Heb. 11:16), nor is Christ ashamed to call believers His brothers (Heb. 2:11). Since God is not ashamed of them, they should not be ashamed of Him. A believer should not be ashamed to confess the name of Christ in salvation (Rom. 10:11), to witness to others about the power of God within the gospel (Rom. 1:16), nor to identify himself with other Christians (II Tim. 1:8).

The inclusive phrase "in nothing" refers to good and bad times, to situations of life or death. In Paul's case, it denoted both freedom and imprisonment.

3. He magnified Christ

Warren Wiersbe says that a believer should be like a microscope so as to make a little Christ appear to be big to an unsaved world, and like a telescope to bring that distant Savior close to it.[2] Jesus Christ is even now in the third heaven at the right hand of the Father, in His resurrected, glorified human body. At the same time, He is spiritually present in the world through His divine attribute of omnipresence and His indwelling presence within the life of each

[2]Warren W. Wiersbe, *Be Joyful*, pp. 37–38.

Christian. The only way that an unsaved person will be able to "see" Christ today is in and through a believer.

In that connection, Paul expressed five features about his magnification of Christ. *First,* its manner was "with all boldness." The idea behind "boldness" *(parrēsia)* is a total freedom of speech before God, friends, and foes (Heb 10:19). He requested prayer that he might open his "mouth boldly to make known the mystery of the gospel" (Eph. 6:19). He wanted to speak boldly as he ought to speak (Eph. 6:20). Christ is thus glorified when believers speak for Him, in what they say, and in how they declare Him.

Second, it was done consistently ("as always, so now"). He did not vacillate. He had magnified Christ through the success of three missionary journeys, and he was not about to change now that he was a prisoner in the very presence of Caesar himself. As a spiritual bride, he had promised to love, honor, and obey his redemptive bridegroom for better, for worse, and in both riches and poverty. He did not permit adverse circumstances to lessen his devotion to the Savior or to decrease his active witness.

In the past, he had forthrightly stood for Christ before sorcerers (Acts 13:8), enraged synagogue Jews (Acts 13:44–45), polytheistic heathen (Acts 14:11–18), Judaizers (Acts 15:1–2), city officials (Acts 16:20–22), philosophers (Acts 17:18–34), and materialistic silversmiths (Acts 19:23–41). After his arrest at Jerusalem, he gave a bold witness five times before the Jewish multitude at the temple (Acts 22:1–24), before the religious council (Acts 23:1–10), at Caesarea before the Roman governors Felix and Festus (Acts 24:1–27), and later before Herod Agrippa II (Acts 26:1–32). During the voyage, the shipwreck, and the subsequent arrival at Rome, the apostle remained constant and steadfast in his testimony (Acts 27–28). In this sense, he manifested the courage of Daniel. When the decree prohibiting prayer was issued, Daniel "went into his house; and his windows being open in his chamber toward Jerusalem, he kneeled upon his knees three times a day, and prayed, and gave thanks before his God, *as he did aforetime*" (Dan. 6:10).

Third, Christ was magnified in Paul by the agency of the Holy Spirit. There is a switch in the verbal structure here.[3] He did not say: "I shall magnify Christ"; rather, he wrote: "Christ shall be magnified." The passive voice suggests that Christ would be magnified by Paul through an outside influence. The apostle was a microscope or a telescope, but the Spirit was the one who controlled the focus of the instrument. The verb "be magnified" means "to be made great" or "to be extolled."[4]

Fourth, its sphere was in the "body." A. T. Robertson observed: "It is harder often to make Christ great in the body than in the spirit."[5] The body, of course, is the arena in which natural life occurs and which death so forcefully attacks. It is the most observable feature of human existence. It is impossible to talk about the magnification of Christ in one's thoughts and feelings without seeing a visible demonstration. People watch what others do and say. There can be no glorification of God in the spirit without the body being involved. The Bible knows of no such dichotomy between man's physical and spiritual constitution. Rather, the exhortation is always directed toward the total man: "For ye are bought with a price: therefore glorify God in your body, and in your spirit, which are God's" (I Cor. 6:20).

Fifth, the magnification of Christ had a double means of accomplishment ("whether it be by life, or by death"). To Paul, death was just as much a means to glorify Christ as was life. Most people view death with a pessimistic, defeatist outlook, but Paul saw it as a victory to be won. He wanted people to say: "Look at how he lived! Look at how he died!" Unfortunately, many believers who have been admired during their lifetimes have lost their testimonies through their predeath depression. Even Peter rebuked Christ when He spoke about the necessity of His death (Matt. 16:21–22).

---

[3]From first person to third person.
[4]The verb "magnified" *(megalunthēsetai)* is based upon the Greek adjective which means "great" *(megas).*
[5]A. T. Robertson, *Word Pictures in the New Testament,* IV, 440.

Later, at the transfiguration, both Moses and Elijah spoke favorably about the decease which Christ would accomplish (Luke 9:31).

B. His Creed (1:21)

The connective "for" *(gar)* gives the explanation for his strong testimony. He had an intense, personal philosophy of life and death. The English prepositional phrase "to me" is actually just one Greek word *(emoi).*[6] In the sentence, it is very emphatic because it stands first and also because it is the emphatic form of the personal pronoun. In effect, he wrote: "Me! As far as I am concerned!" In so doing he did not exclude others from having the same motivation. He just wanted the Philippians to know what his own outlook was.

1. For life

Paul's creed was so simple, yet so profound: "... to live is Christ." Actually, the verb ("is") is not found here. Literally, it reads: "The act of living: Christ." Paul's thoughts, feelings, and actions were fixed on Christ and controlled by Him. The Savior was both the center and the circumference of his daily existence. Paul personified the fulfillment of Christ's ultimate challenge:

> If any man will come after me, let him deny himself, and take up his cross, and follow me.
> For whosoever will save his life shall lose it: and whosoever will lose his life for my sake shall find it (Matt. 16:24–25).

The apostle had both life and the abundant life (John 10:10). He could daily report: "I am crucified with Christ: nevertheless I live; yet not I, but Christ liveth in me: and the life which I now live in the flesh I live by the faith of the Son of God, who loved me, and gave himself for me" (Gal. 2:20). He

---

[6]Dative, singular, first person personal pronoun.

was the ideal branch, clean and yielded to the life of the vine—Christ, who flowed through him (John 15:1–5).

Word association games are often played today. When the name "Jack Nicklaus" is mentioned, avid sports fans think of *golf,* or when the name "Pete Rose" comes up in conversation, *baseball* immediately comes to mind. In the same way, in the first century when the name "Paul" was mentioned, the first name that came to mind was "Christ."

2. For death

Jim Elliot, one of the five missionaries who were martyred by the Auca Indians in the jungles of Ecuador, once said: "He is no fool who loses what he cannot keep to gain that which he cannot lose." Those sentiments echoed Paul's disclaimer of death as an end or a victor ("and to die is gain").

The verbal construction of the phrase "to die" again consists of an article with the aorist infinitive *to apothanein.* The emphasis is upon that split second of time when death actually occurs, when the self is separated from the body. That event is instantaneous, whereas life is constant.[7] The process of death, which is often long and painful, is not contemplated in this concept. When a believer dies, he immediately is free of suffering and is directly present with Christ in the third heaven. From that point on, he will be with the Savior forever. This is the reason why Paul could call the instantaneous act of death "gain" *(kerdos).* Earth's loss is always heaven's gain. The Psalmist wisely declared: "Precious in the sight of the Lord is the death of his saints" (Ps. 116:15).

C. His Choices (1:22–23)

Paul, of course, could not will his death. Solomon declared: "There is no man that hath power over the spirit to retain the spirit; neither hath he power in the day of death" (Eccl. 8:8). Only one person, Jesus Christ, had the delegated authority to

---

[7]Note the contrast between the two tenses of the infinitive. The first is present, whereas the second is aorist.

release his spirit at death and to resurrect himself (John 10:18).

The apostle, however, could express his preferences, leaving the actual choice with a sovereign God. He thus stated the ramifications of two distinct possibilities for his immediate future.

1. To be on earth (1:22)

Three aspects of this possibility are given. *First*, Paul knew that he would continue to live. The usage of the conditional particle *"if" (ei)* does not mean that his future was uncertain; rather, it introduces a condition of reality upon which he could base a conclusion.[8] He said: "But if to live in the flesh is my decreed lot, and it is, then . . . . " The prepositional phrase "in the flesh" denotes life on earth in the natural body; it has no connotation of sinful flesh here (cf. John 1:14; II Cor. 10:3).

Second, Paul knew that his ministry would be successful. The demonstrative pronoun "this" refers to the continuation of his natural life.[9] To Paul, living meant more working, and more working meant more fruit bearing. Although he was advanced in age and exhausted after three tiring missionary journeys and several recent imprisonments, he claimed the promise: "They shall still bring forth fruit in old age; they shall be fat and flourishing" (Ps. 92:14).

The "fruit of my labor" specifically applied to the results of his missionary activity. It included the salvation of sinners, the edification of saints, the establishment of churches, the training of new leaders, and the writing of inspired Scripture. He informed the Romans that he wanted to "have some fruit among [them] also, even as among other Gentiles" (Rom. 1:13). The apostle expected to share this fruit with others be-

---

[8]The usage of *ei* with the indicative verbal mood introduces a condition true to reality (cf. Col. 3:1). Although no verb is actually found in this clause, one must be implied.

[9]It is neuter *(touto)* and points back to the articular infinitive, which has a neuter article *(to)*.

cause those who supported him financially had made an investment in his ministry which would bring to them the dividends of fruit (4:17).

Third, he did not disclose his personal preference ("yet what I shall choose, I wot not"). The old English verb "wot not" is more easily translated today as "I do not make known" *(ou gnōrizō).* Death would be a personal gain to him, but an extended ministry also had value, both for him and others. He knew what course he would choose for his life if he would have had that prerogative, but he determined not to reveal his inner feelings to others.

2. To be in heaven (1:23)

Most people want life without death rather than life with death. The natural desire of humans is to live, not to die. Those who choose death over life usually want relief from suffering or depression. The case of Paul, however, was much different. He had to determine where he wanted to live. Today, people make choices about living in the city or in the country, and about residing in the north or in the sun belt. The apostle debated the advantages and disadvantages of living on earth with living in heaven; thus, his approach toward death was unique.

Three reasons are given why he preferred heaven. *First,* it was an inner compulsion ("For I am in a strait betwixt two"). The verb literally means "to have with" *(sunechomai).* It referred to pressure being imposed upon someone from two different directions, to be hemmed in on both sides. The apostle used it in regard to the constraint of the love of Christ which motivated his ministry (II Cor. 5:14; cf. Acts 18:5). Christ used the same term to describe the pressure upon Him as He faced the cross: "But I have a baptism to be baptized with; and how am I straitened till it be accomplished." (Luke 12:50). The "two" constraints that pushed at Paul were the necessity to abide and the desire to depart. Both compulsions were valid and equally strong.

Second, it was a "desire." This noun, often translated as "lust" (Gal. 5:16–17), describes an inner passion or drive. It actually appears with the article (*tēn epithumian*, "the desire"), making it even more intense.[10]

This desire was no mere whim. The verb "having"[11] shows that it was a constant part of Paul's inner feelings at this time in his life. It would be difficult to say whether this desire also possessed him in the younger years of his ministry, but both age and physical exhaustion had quickened his interest in heaven.

The desire had a single purpose with two aspects.[12] He first wanted "to depart." This unusual verb *(analusai)* is used of the unloosing of prisoners, the removal of the yoke from an ox after the day's work, the breaking up of a tent or an encampment, and the loosing of a ship from its moorings. The human body is often described as a tent or a tabernacle (John 1:14; II Cor. 5:1); thus death would be the breaking down of one tent in order to move on to a new location. Later, when the apostle did expect to die during his second Roman imprisonment, he confessed that the time of his "departure" *(analuseōs)* was at hand (II Tim. 4:6). Second, he wanted "to be with Christ." Thus death was not an escape or a "copout"; rather, it meant that he would be with the most important person in his life. The verb indicates eternal fellowship *(einai)*.[13] Death is instantaneous, but life with Christ is forever. Elsewhere, he wrote:

> Therefore we are always confident, knowing that, while we are at home in the body, we are absent from the Lord:
> (For we walk by faith, not by sight:)
> We are confident, I say, and willing rather to be absent from the body, and to be present with the Lord (II Cor. 5:6–8).

---

[10]The emphasis is further strengthened by the fact that it appears first in the sentence, even before the verb.

[11]Present active participle.

[12]Indicated by the Greek construction: *eis to analusai kai ... einai*. The purpose preposition *eis* is followed by one article *to* which joins two infinitives.

[13]It is a present infinitive, whereas the infinitive for departure is aorist.

The Bible says nothing about a soulsleep after death or a temporary residency in purgatory. Right now, a believer is on earth; at death, he immediately goes into the presence of Jesus Christ.

Third, it was "far better." Actually, there are three comparative adjectives in this phrase *(pollōi mallon kreisson).* Literally, it reads "much more better." In quantity, quality, or any other comparative values, heaven is far superior to earth. In fact, there can be no comparison.

D. His Concern (1:24)

The inner struggle was whether to depart or to abide. Paul's preference for heaven and Christ, though sincere and holy, manifested a slight selfishness. After all, Paul was foremost a servant, and a servant must live to meet the needs of others (1:1). He knew what he wanted to do, but he also recognized what he had to do.

Three aspects of Paul's concern are enumerated. *First,* he accepted the fact that he would "abide in the flesh." The verb means "to remain upon" *(epimenein).*[14] Thus, he planned to remain upon the earth in his natural body. He gave no indication that he would die then or in the immediate future.

Second, his continued living was "more needful" *(anagkaioteron).* A person who makes decisions out of love and humility will always do what is best for others, not what is best for himself. In this fashion, Paul could again prove himself to be an example to them.

Third, he wanted to abide for them ("for you"). The benefit for them will be explained in the next two verses. Since he had them in his heart (1:7), he had to think of them when he contemplated his own personal future.

---

[14]It is another articular infinitive *to epimenein.*

THE BLESSINGS OF LIFE AND DEATH
II. FOR THE PHILIPPIANS (1:25-26)

There was value to Paul in either his life or death, but the Philippians would only receive benefit if the apostle should live. That factor alone gave the apostle an inner conviction that he would be spared from a Roman death ("and having this confidence"; cf. 1:6). He knew that his return to active missionary service would produce two major blessings for the church.

A. The Increase of Faith (1:25)

1. His knowledge

Paul knew intuitively by the indelible conviction of the Holy Spirit that he would be set free ("I know," *oida*). This verb stresses an innate knowledge in contrast to an experiential, learned wisdom *(ginōskō)*. There were no objective criteria produced by the trials themselves which would have caused the apostle to have a glimmer of hope. He viewed the imprisonment and legal appeals from the standpoint of the divine will and human necessity.

His knowledge manifested itself in two predictions. *First,* he knew that he would remain alive ("I shall abide," *menō*). *Second,* he knew that he would return to Philippi ("continue with you"). This verb literally means "to remain with them beside them" *(sumparamenō)*. It was one thing to get out of prison; it was another to be able to travel to their city once again.

2. Their faith

The word "for" *(eis)* introduces the reason behind his release. Two results could be achieved.[15] *First,* their faith would advance ("your furtherance ... of faith"). Just as adverse circumstances furthered the outreach of the gospel

---

[15]Actually, it is one result with two features. The Granville Sharp rule is again seen here. The two nouns, serving as the objects of the preposition, have only one article to designate them: *eis tēn humōn prokopēn kai charan.*

(1:12), so the good news of the apostle's release would increase their faith in God who can redeem men from all difficulty.

Second, their faith would be full of "joy." Faith must not only be intellectual and volitional, it must also be emotional. Belief must cause tears of happiness. Jeremiah's proclamations of doom against Jerusalem demonstrated a faith without joy: an anticipating faith, however, should shout and sing at the fulfillment of redemption. When faith becomes married to sight, joy will officiate.

B. The Joy of Reunion (1:26)

Friends and loved ones are often taken for granted until they are gone. When death separates, it is too late for statements and gifts of love and gratitude. Quite often a severe accident or a strickening illness serves to stimulate expressions of sensitivity. The sorrow of possible loss is quickly replaced by the joy of reunion when the loved one returns home.

In similar fashion, Paul saw four possible features of their rejoicing. *First,* it would be "more abundant" *(perisseuēi).* It would be full and running over constantly. *Second,* it would rest "in Jesus Christ." He would get the glory and praise for what had been accomplished. *Third,* it would also reside in Paul ("for me"). Literally, it reads "in me" *(en emoi).* A believer can rejoice at the presence of another believer and of the omnipresent Savior at the same time. Such rejoicing is complementary, not contradictory. *Fourth,* it would be caused by Paul's personal return ("by my coming to you again").[16] Both the return of Epaphroditus and the visit of Timothy would not generate the joy that the physical presence of the apostle in their midst would produce.

---

[16]The verbal noun "coming," often used of Christ's return, literally means "to be beside" *(parousias).*

THE BLESSINGS OF LIFE AND DEATH

Questions for Discussion

1. In what ways are some Christians ashamed today? What can help them to correct this weakness?

2. Can speaking boldly be done improperly? How? How does courtesy fit into one's witness?

3. Are believers consistent? Why do they have highs and lows in their experience? Is constancy a mark of leadership?

4. How can Christ be magnified in the home? At school? At work?

5. What is the first thing that comes into a person's mind when he hears your name? For what do you want to be known?

6. Do all Christians have a healthy outlook toward death? How can a believer fail Christ in his death? In his funeral? In his will?

7. What are the values of separation? Of reunion? Can such lessons be learned apart from hard human experience?

The Challenge to the Church
Philippians 1:27—2:4

In the opening portion of this epistle, Paul dealt mainly with events that affected his own behavior. He then turned his attention to the spiritual condition of the Philippians. From Epaphroditus and subsequent church messengers,[1] the apostle realized that the church needed encouragement and exhortation. In this passage, he develops his instruction around two basic appeals (1:27; 2:2).[2]

I. BE GOOD CITIZENS OF HEAVEN (1:27–30)

Some unsaved inhabitants of this world have developed a distaste for heaven because of the shoddy behavior of "ugly" Christians in their midst. Such improper actions must be stopped. To accomplish these ends, believers must know who they are and what they must do.

A. Definition of Citizenship (1:27a)

1. The believer is a citizen of heaven

The exhortation "let your conversation be" is better translated: "Behave constantly as citizens." The Greek verb

---

[1]A report came later, notifying Paul that the church knew about the sickness of Epaphroditus (2:26).

[2]The two imperatives are *politeuesthe* (1:27) and *plērōsate* (2:2). The rest of the material is subordinate to these two main verbs.

(politeuesthe) comes from the word for *city (polis)*, found within the names of several American cities[3] and which transliterates into the English term "politics." The Philippians understood this term well because they were constituted as a Roman colony within the province of Macedonia. They thus were free Roman citizens, possessing all of the rights and privileges thereof (cf. Acts 22:28). They knew that they represented Rome in the midst of a Greek culture and land.

In his defense before the Jerusalem council, Paul used this same term of himself: "I have lived [*pepoliteumai*] in all good conscience before God until this day" (Acts 23:1). All believers have heavenly citizenship (3:20).[4] The Philippian Christians were never citizens of the covenant nation Israel (Eph. 2:12), but they were now "fellow citizens with the saints, and of the household of God" (Eph. 2:19).

2. *The believer must be a worthy citizen*

The adverbial phrase "as it becometh" is a translation of one Greek word *(axiōs)*, normally read as "worthy." The apostle exhorted the Ephesians to "walk worthy of the vocation" wherewith they were called (Eph. 4:1). He challenged the Colossians to "walk worthy of the Lord unto all pleasing" (Col. 1:10). The Thessalonians were to "walk worthy of God," who had called them into his kingdom and glory (I Thess. 2:12).

This aspect of the citizenship is the main emphasis in this verse.[5] A worthy walk recognizes the double citizenship of every believer. Paul admitted his Roman citizenship and used those rights at times (Acts 22:28; 25:10); but such citizenship is temporary, limited to this life. He also knew that he was primarily a citizen of heaven, a position which

---

[3]For example, Indianapolis and Minneapolis.

[4]The word "conversation" is really "citizenship" *(politeuma)*.

[5]The adverb actually occurs first in the sentence, after the connective "only."

would never end. Worthy citizenship therefore involves obligations to both human governments and God (Matt. 22:21).

3. *The believer must represent the gospel*

The behavior of a heavenly citizen must be worthy of "the gospel of Christ." All Christians are Christ's ambassadors to bring the good news of divine reconciliation to a lost and hostile world (II Cor. 5:20). They therefore should do nothing to antagonize the very people that God is trying to save. They must not give offense (I Cor. 10:32–33). They must further the outreach of the gospel by their presence, influence, speech, and actions.

4. *The believer must be a devoted citizen*

A good citizen will behave properly, with or without supervision. Therefore, Paul's presence ("whether I come and see you") or absence ("or else be absent") should have nothing to do with the way they should live. Regardless, their behavior was to be constant. After all, they were ultimately responsible to God who was always watching them.

In factories, foremen are necessary to motivate workers to attain their goals and deadlines. Unfortunately, when the foreman leaves the work area, many workers relax and diminish their productivity. On the contrary, Christians should be so devoted to Christ and to their moral responsibilities that they will not labor "with eyeservice, as menpleasers; but in singleness of heart, fearing God" (Col. 3:22).

B. Goals of Citizenship (1:27b–30)

The aim of heavenly citizenship is steadfast living on earth ("that ye stand fast"). The verb tense indicates that they were to maintain their stand throughout their earthly residency.[6] Some believers, unfortunately, do nothing else but stand fast. They do not work for the Lord. There are others who work

---

[6]Present active indicative.

but do not stand. Here are five characteristics of the God-pleasing stand.

1. Stand in unity (1:27b)

They were to stand "in one spirit" *(en heni pneumati).* The "spirit" may refer to the Holy Spirit or to the oneness of purpose created within the human spirit by the Holy Spirit. There can be no unity within the brethren apart from the sovereign control of the Spirit.

All believers have been equally baptized in that one Spirit into the body of Christ, the true Church (I Cor. 12:13), have drunk by faith of the Spirit (I Cor. 12:13), are indwelt by Him (I Cor. 6:19–20), and have access by Him unto the Father (Eph. 2:18). They must endeavor "to keep the unity of the Spirit in the bond of peace," a unity marked by one body, one Spirit, one hope, one Lord, one faith, one baptism, and one God and Father of all (Eph. 4:3–6).

2. Stand in evangelism (1:27c)

Three marks of this purpose are given. *First,* they needed "one mind." Literally, it reads "one soul" *(miāi psuchēi).* Their souls were to be joined together, even as David and Jonathan loved each other (I Sam. 18:1). The soul is the seat of desires and emotions, whereas the spirit is the center of thought.

Second, they needed to strive together; they were to co-operate as teammates. The word *athlete* comes from the Greek verb translated as "striving together" *(sunathlountes).* In pro football, the offensive and the defensive units must complement each other. They must encourage each other, but they should not blame one another. The backfield and the line must be synchronized to achieve a common goal.

Each believer must execute his own assignment. Paul, however, cautioned: "And if a man also strive [same word] for masteries, yet is he not crowned, except he strive lawfully" (II Tim. 2:5). Effort must be expended in the right time and way. An athlete must carry out the instructions of the play designed by the coach. When all of the athletes carry out their tasks, then there will be team success.

Third, their goal was "the faith of the gospel." Like a good defensive team, they must not let Satan and false teachers penetrate. Like a good offensive team, they must drive forward to victory. They must defend the truth and win converts at the same time.

The phrase "the faith" *(tēi pistei)* has the definite article and thus points to the specific body of spiritual truth that the local church must preserve and propagate (I Tim. 3:15). Paul predicted that some would depart from the faith (I Tim. 4:1). Jude encouraged his readers to "contend for the faith which was once delivered unto the saints (Jude 3).

The entire phrase points to all of the truth necessary to be understood and to be believed for salvation. It includes a clear biblical exposition of the redemptive work of Jesus Christ.

3. Stand without fear (1:28)

The opening phrase "the faith of the gospel" reinforces the manner of their stand ("and in nothing terrified by your adversaries")[7]. The verb "terrified" *(pturomenoi)* was used of horses that were frightened or spooked into an uncontrollable stampede. Inner fear is usually caused by an outside stimulus.

Double citizenship has advantages, but it also brings misunderstanding and conflict. A believer is in the kingdom of God, but he also lives among the kingdoms of the world which is ruled by Satan (Luke 4:5–6).

The "adversaries" of the Philippians included the Romans who thought that Christians were atheists because they had no images of God, the Judaizers (3:2), the idolaters, the evil world system, and Satan. Such opposition could cause even the strongest believer to tremble, but Jesus admonished: "Be not afraid of them that kill the body" (Luke 12:4). He an-

---

[7]The word "terrified" is a participle and must be joined to the understood subject of the verb "stand" (ye).

nounced that tribulation would come, but He also declared that He had overcome the world (John 16:33).

Such opposition must be seen for what it really is. It has two sides. *First,* it is "to them an evident token of perdition." The phrase "evident token" *(endeixis)* is an ancient legal term for a demonstrable proof. The hostility of the opponents revealed the fact that they were unsaved and that they would receive the judgment of God because of their unbelief and unrighteous persecution of believers. Their sinful practice manifested their sinful position before God. The concept behind "perdition" *(apōleias)* is that of lostness, the very antithesis of salvation.

Second, deliberate adversity is to believers a proof "of salvation." The world loves its own, but it hates and persecutes those who have defected to God (John 15:18–19). In one sense, a Christian should rejoice when opposition comes because he can conclude that the world sees Christ in him. This alone can give him assurance that he is genuinely saved. The qualifying phrase "and that of God" shows that God is the source of salvation and that He has permitted the persecution to occur within limits prescribed by Him.

4. Stand in suffering (1:29)

Persecution by the world affords the believer an opportunity to suffer for the sake of righteousness (Matt. 5:10). Jesus said:

> Blessed are ye, when men shall revile you, and persecute you, and shall say all manner of evil against you falsely, for my sake.
>
> Rejoice, and be exceeding glad: for great is your reward in heaven: for so persecuted they the prophets which were before you (Matt. 5:11–12).

Persecution by the world should not be viewed as a punishment but as a gift ("For unto you it is given in the behalf of Christ"). The verb *echaristhē* is based upon the word for "grace" *(charis)*. Since grace is unmerited divine favor, men do not deserve to suffer for Christ any more than they deserve to be saved through Him. After their first beating by the Jewish elders, the apostles rejoiced "that they were counted worthy to suffer shame for His name" (Acts 5:41).

The two divine gifts imparted to all believers are listed in chronological order. *First*, it was given to them "to believe on him." Salvation is of the Lord, from the beginning to the end (Jonah 2:9). As the object of divine choice, the believer knows that he will be in heaven because of what Christ has done for him, not because of what he has done for Christ. All will agree: "For by grace are ye saved through faith; and that not of yourselves: it is the gift of God: Not of works, lest any man should boast" (Eph. 2:8–9). The entire program of salvation, including faith and grace, is a gift from a loving God.

Second, it was given to them "also to suffer for his sake." Most Christians are like Peter in his earlier discipleship. They want the glory of the kingdom without the sufferings of the cross. They do not consider any suffering to be a gift. They want faith without conflict. These reactions show a great lack in their understanding of God's dealings with His children. Suffering for Christ brings assurance (I Peter 4:14), rewards (I Peter 4:13), men to Christ (1:12–14), and glory to God (Acts 9:16).

A distinction must be made between suffering per se and Christian suffering. A believer must suffer "for his sake." It literally reads "in behalf of him" *(huper autou)*. Just as Christ once suffered for the believer, so the child of God should suffer for Him. The believer must follow Christ's example (I Peter 2:21). Suffering for wrongdoing or stupid mistakes is deserved and will bring no reward (I Peter 2:19–20).

5. *Stand with Paul (1:30)*

The church was experiencing "the same conflict" with Paul. The term "conflict" *(agōna)* transliterates as "agony." It was used of the strenuous struggles of athletic and gladiatorial contests. The same word is used in the apostle's charge to Timothy: "Fight the good fight [agōna] of faith"

(I Tim. 6:12).[8] At the end of his life, Paul confessed: "I have fought a good fight [agōna]" (II Tim. 4:7). The Christian life is not easy; it is a war, a battle, a wrestling match. The believer wrestles "not against flesh and blood, but against principalities, against powers, against the rulers of the darkness of this world, against spiritual wickedness in high places" (Eph. 6:12). The conflict is with Satan as he employs devious methods through demons and unregenerate men (Eph. 6:11). To stand, the believer must put on the defensive armor of God (Eph. 6:10–18).

This conflict resembles Paul's in two ways. *First,* it was like that which Paul endured at Philippi during his initial evangelization of the city ("which ye saw in me;" cf. Acts 16:19–40). They saw what happened to him, namely, his beatings and imprisonment. They saw his spiritual response to the sufferings and the shameful treatment (I Thess. 2:2).

Second, it was like that which Paul was presently experiencing in Rome ("and now hear to be in me"). The church only had secondhand reports of the apostle's predicament. Epaphroditus was therefore dispatched to gain firsthand information. Just as Paul wanted to enter into the fellowship of Christ's sufferings, so he reminded the Philippian believers that they had begun to share in his spiritual conflicts. This action should bring praise and support, not pessimism and self-pity.

II. BRING JOY TO PAUL (2:1–4)

The Philippians lost some of their joy when they heard about the arrest and the subsequent imprisonments of Paul. Their joy was further lessened when they heard about the terminal sickness of Epaphroditus (2:26–28). They were totally unaware that Paul was rejoicing in the midst of his adversity. They wanted the apostle to have joy; but instead, they themselves were in need of it.

[8]Both the imperative and the direct object are based upon the same stem: *agōnizou ... agōna.* Cf. II Tim. 4:7.

The apostle, of course, could not have total joy as long as the church was marked by sadness. In addition, when believers are not rejoicing in the Lord they will be marked by divisiveness, pride, and selfishness. To correct the situation, Paul issued a direct command: "Fulfil ye my joy" (2:2). The imperative could also be translated: "Fill full my joy" *(plērō-sate)*.[9] The Philippians had filled Paul's life with joy through their salvation, devotion to the Lord, and financial support; however, that joy over their spiritual condition had been diminished by their growing disunity. Now they needed to replenish what had evaporated from the apostle's cup of joy.

A. Conditions for Joy (2:1)

Joy is based upon attitudes and relationships. Paul could not have joy if the Philippian's attitude was right toward him but wrong toward others.

He set forth four grounds for joy. They are marked by the fourfold usages of "if" *(ei)* and "any" *(tis, ti, tina)*. Grammatically, they are four conditional clauses that assume the reality of the statement.[10] The continuity between this section of verses and the previous one is indicated by the connective "therefore" *(oun)*.

1. Consolation in Christ

The word "consolation" *(paraklēsis)* can refer either to an exhortation or to the comfort produced by that appeal. As comfort, it is both an attribute of God and a gift from Him (John 14:16; II Cor. 1:3–4; 7:4). As exhortation, it becomes the ground of appeal for Paul. As an apostle, he besought them to obey the prayerful injunction of Christ: "That they all may be one: as thou, Father, art in me, and I in thee, that they also may be one in us" (John 17:21). There can be no

---

[9]Aorist active imperative.

[10]The verb "is" and the conclusion are implied. For example: If there is any consolation in Christ, and there is, then fulfill my joy.

real joy when warring believers fail to obey the command of Christ to be one.

2. Comfort of love

The "comfort of love" will produce joy and unity when believers love Christ as they should and when they love one another as Christ has loved them (John 13:34–35). Lack of assurance of salvation and lack of effective witness are both caused when believers fail to love one another.

The term "comfort" *(paramuthion)* conveys the idea of persuasive address, incentive, or stimulus. It is used in the command: "Comfort the feebleminded" (I Thess. 5:14). This needy person is literally a "little soul" *(oligopsuchous)*. Acting out of love *(agapēs)*, a believer will encourage the depressed Christian with his words of comfort, his friendship, and his deeds of mercy.

3. Communion of Spirit

All believers share in the "fellowship of the Spirit" *(koinōnia pneumatos)*. The Holy Spirit dwells in each of them, and He joins them all within the one body of Christ. Genuine submission to Him will produce the fruit of the Spirit, which is "love, joy, peace, longsuffering, gentleness, goodness, faith, meekness, temperance" (Gal. 5:22–23).

4. Compassion

The two sides of brotherly compassion are seen in the compound phrase "bowels and mercies." The term "bowels" *(splagchna)* referred to the inner organs of the body, which indicated the seat of human emotions. The concept "mercies" *(oiktirmoi)* pointed to the outward deeds of mercy caused by the inner concern. Compassion is the opposite of indifference. Where there is no compassion, there can be no love nor joy (I John 3:16–18).

B. Nature of Joy (2:2–4)

Paul directs this admonition to the Philippian believers, "Fulfill ye my joy." Joy is not mere laughter or a happy smile. Happiness can be manufactured, but joy must be grown. It involves time and obedience. Three of its essential qualities are expressed here.

1. Unity (2:2)

The conjunction "that" *(hina)* can denote either purpose or content.[11] The latter is more plausible here. Four descriptions of the unity are given. *First,* they were to be "like-minded." The phrase literally reads: "that you keep on thinking the same thing" *(hina to auto phronēte).* The same expression is used later of Euodias and Syntyche who needed to be "of the same mind in the Lord" (4:2). The "same thing" is doubtless the glorification of God through joint evangelistic effort and holy thought patterns (1:27; 4:8).

Second, they needed to have "the same love." Believers must be united in love; they must love whom and what God loves. They must love each other with the same love. They must love God with their total beings, their neighbors as themselves, and their spiritual brothers as Christ sacrificially loved them (Matt. 22:37–39; John 13:34).

Third, they had to be "of one accord." This phrase literally means "joint souls" *(sumpsuchoi).* As a chain, one soul must be linked together with another soul. No Christian can function independently; rather, he must live in harmony with both Christ and other believers.

Fourth, they must be "of one mind." Literally, it translates: "thinking constantly the one thing" *(to hen phronountes).*[12] The "one thing" is later explained as the selfless mind of Christ (2:5). It could also include the single-minded purpose

---

[11] When "purpose," it is translated "in order that," and when "explanatory," simply "that."

[12] Same verb as in the first phrase ("likeminded").

of pressing "toward the mark for the prize of the high calling of God in Christ Jesus" (3:14). Robertson claims that believers should be "like clocks that strike at the same moment."[13]

2. Humility (2:3)

Wiersbe states that "humility is that grace that, when you know you have it, you have lost it."[14] In this passage, Paul viewed the joy of humility as both a negative and a positive quality.

Negatively, believers should not possess a selfish, competitive spirit. The opening words read "nothing according to strife or vainglory" *(mēden kata eritheian ē kenodoxian).*[15] Someone has said that vainglory is the disease whereas strife is the symptom. The former is inward and the latter is outward.

The sin of "strife" *(eritheian)* is a work of the flesh (Gal. 5:20). It characterized those who preached out of a faulty motivation (1:15). It incorporates party squabbles and petty conceits. It marked the disciples as they argued over which of them was the greatest (Luke 22:24). It caused James, John, and their mother to request the two thrones closest to that of Christ's (Matt. 20:20–28; Mark 10:35–45).

The concept behind "vainglory" *(kenodoxian)* is that it is an empty glory. In appearance it may seem to be spiritually impressive, but inside there is no substance. It is like a balloon; the larger it stretches on the outside, the bigger the emptiness on the inside. The Pharisees had it when they prayed, gave, and fasted before men to have the glory of men (Matt. 6:1–18). Diotrephes had it when he strived to attain preeminence within the church (III John 9).

Positively, believers should have a high opinion of others. This does not mean that Christians should have a poor self-image; rather, they should try to lift others up without

---

[13]A. T. Robertson, *Word Pictures,* IV, 443.

[14]Warren W. Wiersbe, *Be Joyful,* p. 50.

[15]Note that the words "let . . . be done" are in italics. They are not found in the Greek text.

exalting themselves. They must have the servant mind, humbling themselves in order to serve others. They must not think of themselves more highly than they ought to think (Rom. 12:3). They should recognize that they are what they are by the grace of God (I Cor. 15:10). True humility will rejoice in what God has made of them and what He has done through them (I Cor. 1:26–31; 4:6–7). Jesus said to the competitive disciples: Whosoever will be great among you, let him be your minister; and whosoever will be chief among you, let him be your servant" (Matt. 20:26–27). To a Christian, the way up must always be the way down (cf. I Peter 5:5–6).

3. Concern for others (2:4)

The admonition was both inclusive (plural verb) and individual ("every man;" *hekastos*). The verb "look" *(skopeite)* is the basis of the English word *scope*. It means to keep one's eye constantly focused on an object. Two such possibilities exist.

First, a believer should look not only "on his own things." This phrase is greatly emphasized, occurring first in the sentence. He should not have a selfish outlook. He should not be looking out only for his own interests, saying: What is in it for me? What will I get out of it?

Second, a believer should look "on the things of others." The adversative "but" *(alla)* is very emphatic, showing the contrast between selfishness and selflessness. He should ask: What are the needs of my brother? What can I do to help him? Elsewhere, the apostle wrote:

> We then that are strong ought to bear the infirmities of the weak, and not to please ourselves.
> Let everyone of us please his neighbor for his good to edification (Rom. 15:1–2).

THE CHALLENGE TO THE CHURCH

Questions for Discussion

1. In what ways do believers manifest that they are good citizens of heaven?

2. Are Christians consistent? Should they be faithful in church attendance when they are away on vacation? Should Christian college students observe the school regulations when they are home for the summer?

3. Should Christians cooperate in evangelistic efforts with all others regardless of moral and doctrinal differences?

4. In what ways do believers fear spiritual opposition? Physical? Social? How can they be encouraged?

5. In what practical ways can believers manifest unity? What is the difference between conformity and unity? Unity and union?

6. What are the marks of pride? Of humility? Of concern for others? Do modern church programs foster vainglory?

The Humiliation and Exaltation of Christ
Philippians 2:5–11

The perfect example of servanthood is Jesus Christ. In Him can be seen the manifestation of unity, humility, and concern for others.

The explanatory connective "for" *(gar)*[1] joins the exhortations to the church with the example of Christ. In so doing, Paul has contributed one of the greatest Christological passages in the entire Bible (cf. John 1:1–14; Col. 1:15–19; Heb. 1:1–3). Paradoxically, he illustrated exhortation with doctrine, whereas most preachers try to make their doctrinal sermons practical.

I. THE ILLUSTRATION OF CHRIST (2:5)

A. The Command

The command literally reads: "Let this (attitude) be minded in you over and over." The present imperative *(phroneisthō)*[2] shows that a humble, altruistic concern must be a daily practice and that it must originate within a submissive will which is determined to obey God. It is not something which God develops within the life of a Christian

---

[1] Not translated in the KJV.
[2] Some Greek texts have *phroneite* (second person plural).

without his knowledge. It is also not achieved through a non-repeatable crisis decision. This same verb was used twice earlier in the appeal for unity: "likeminded" *(to auto phronēte)* and "one mind" *(to hen phronountes)*. The concept behind the verb is that of a mind fixed on a specific purpose, not that of a casual thought.

The demonstrative "this" *(touto)* refers back to the content of the exhortations (2:1–4). This joyful outlook includes unity, humility, and the welfare of others. It also looks forward to the descriptive relative clause introduced by the relative pronoun "which" *(ho).*[3] Paul wanted this proper attitude, which Christ possesses, to be incorporated into the decisions and actions of the church. The prepositional phrase "in you" *(en humin)* is plural. The appeal, therefore, was to the entire assembly, although it had to be carried out by each individual. There can be no church unity or joy if some believers are disobedient.

B. The Example

The relative clause ("which was also in Christ Jesus") provides the link between the command (2:5a) and the theological pattern of Christ (note the word "who;" 2:6). Actually, there is no expressed verb in the clause. The predicate "was" has been supplied and looks back at the historical situation in which Christ displayed His humility. The verb "is" could also have been inserted. This addition would mean that Christ, even in His exalted state, still has the mind of a servant. In the context, the former seems to be more likely, although the truth of the second view cannot be denied.

Christ is often seen in the Scriptures as the supreme example. In the approach to suffering, He has left the believers a pattern which they should follow in His steps (I Peter 2:21). The imagery is that of a child placing his feet into the footprints made by his father during a trek through the snow.

---

[3]Both "this" and "which" are in the neuter gender.

John declared: "He that saith he abideth in him ought himself also to walk, even as he walked" (I John 2:6). Believers should follow Christian leaders who in turn are following Christ (I Cor. 11:1; I Thess. 1:6). After Jesus washed the feet of the disciples, He explained: "For I have given you an example, that ye should do as I have done to you" (John 13:15). Theory must be put into practice, and Jesus Christ has provided the best example in that pursuit.

II. THE HUMILIATION OF CHRIST (2:6–8)

The world often looks at humiliation as forced embarassment. One dictionary cited this usage: "Mother was humiliated by finding that she did not have enough food for her guests." Thus, to them it means to lower the pride or self-respect, to humble, and to mortify.

Christ, however, has elevated the concept to a positive, holy virtue which should be cultivated in the lives of all men. He completely manifested it through His incarnation, earthly ministry, and subsequent death on the cross.

A. His Deity (2:6)

A sovereign God cannot be humbled, because there is no one or nothing outside of Himself that could force Him into that situation; however, He could humble Himself as a free choice of His will. The marvel of the redemptive program is that He did just that: God humbled Himself before man. Humility may seem to be foreign to a superior being, but it actually is an essential attribute of God the Son.

1. He was in the form of God

The phrase "in the form of God" (en morphēi theou) refers to the basic essence of the divine being. It denotes the inner nature, not the external appearance. Muller defines it as "His divine nature, which is inseparable from His person and in which the Divine Being realizes Himself in His immanent, inherent, divine glory and godly attributes."[4] All that God is, Jesus Christ was, is and ever shall be. What can be said about the Son can also be expressed of both the Father and the Holy Spirit. The Father is God, the Son is God, and the Spirit is God; and yet there is only one God (Deut. 6:4). God is a trinitarian oneness. The Christian does not worship three gods, nor are the three persons simply three parts of the one God. There are three distinct persons within the divine being, and yet there is an intrapersonal oneness.

The participle "being" *(huparchōn)* literally means "under beginning" *(hupo* and *archē)*. It denotes prior existence. At the time of the verbal action of this verse ("thought"), He already was existing as God. He did not begin to be in the form of God, because as God he was from eternity in the form of God. John wrote: "In the beginning [archēi][5] was the Word, and the Word was with God, and the Word was God" (John 1:1). To say that Jesus was God and that He was in the form of God is to say the same truth.

2. *He was equal to God*

Christ was not the most God-conscious man who ever lived, nor was He simply like God; rather, He was "equal with God." Christ's equality to God extended to all of the essential attributes. The Son is just as holy, omnipotent, omniscient, and sovereign as the Father.

Even in His incarnate state, the Son could claim: "I and my Father are one" (John 10:30). He asserted that God was His Father in a sense in which He is not the Father of anyone else. They shared the same nature within an eternal relationship. The Jews understood this claim but rejected it totally, charging him with blasphemy: "Therefore the Jews sought the more to kill him, because he not only had broken the sabbath, but said also that God was his Father, making himself equal with God" (John 5:18 cf. 10:33).

---

[4]Jac. J. Muller, *The Epistles of Paul to the Philippians and to Philemon,* pp. 78–79.

[5]This word is contained in the verb "being."

The articular infinitive "to be" *(to einai)* shows again that He always was equal to God. If the apostle wanted to show that Christ desired to become equal to God, he would have used a different verb *(genesthai)*.

3. *He did not selfishly grasp His deity*

The enigmatic phrase "thought it not robbery" can more easily be translated: "Who ... did not consider the fact of being equal to God a prize to be selfishly grasped." The verb "thought" *(hēgēsato)*[6] looks at a logical time in the past when God the Son made a decisive resolution to surrender the divine prerogative to be served in order to serve the human race as its Savior. It is the same verb used of believers who should "esteem others better than themselves" (2:3).

The word "robbery" *(harpagmon)* has both an active and a passive meaning.[7] As active, it would refer to the act of seizing or grasping, whereas the passive would emphasize the result of grasping. The active would imply that He wanted to become equal with God,[8] but the passive looks at the equality as a prize already held. In this context, the passive is the theological preference.

When Christ did not esteem His equality with God as a prized possession, He did not look "on his own things" (cf. 2:4). Instead, He viewed "the things of others," namely, the sinful plight of the human race. He did not contemplate what He would gain for Himself, but rather what He could do for others.

B. His Incarnation (2:7)

The strong adversative "but" *(alla)* contrasts Christ's refusal to be proud as God with His willingness to be humble

---

[6]Aorist middle indicative, deponent.

[7]Usually, nouns which end in *-mos* are active, and these in *ma* are passive; but there are exceptions: e.g. *phragmos* is a fence, not the act of fencing in.

[8]The sect of Jehovah's Witnesses embraces the active position.

as man. The prior verse (2:6) gave his attitude, whereas this verse describes His action. His incarnation is denoted by one main verb ("made of no reputation") which is further explained by two participles ("took" and "was made").

1. He emptied himself

The English phrase ("made himself of no reputation") is actually the translation of two Greek words *(heauton ekenōse)*. Literally, it means: "Himself He emptied."[9] This points to the historical event of the conception when God the Son entered into the body of the virgin Mary, who was completely overshadowed by the ministry of the Holy Spirit at that time.

Of what did He empty Himself? Several views have been put forth. *First,* some claim that He gave up His deity when He became man; however, God cannot diminish His being. He cannot become less than what he is. He is immutable (Mal. 3:6).

Second, others assert that He emptied Himself of His relative attributes, defined as omnipresence, omnipotence, and omniscience. It is true that Christ went through normal human experiences such as learning (Luke 2:52), exhaustion (John 4:6), and geographical, bodily limitation. However, this does not mean that He did not possess these essential characteristics of deity. Today, there is a resurrected, glorified human body in the third heaven, and yet Christ is able to indwell every believer spiritually. (Col. 1:27) and to accompany all believers everywhere (Matt. 28:20).

Third, some state that Christ did not use His divine attributes when He lived on earth; this is not true, however. He created food, walked on water, and forgave sins.

Fourth, the proper explanation that Christ surrendered the independent exercise of His divine attributes. In the incarnation, He yielded His will to that of the Father. He was God manifest in the flesh. Therefore He possessed the attributes,

[9]Emphasis is placed upon the reflexive pronoun which serves as the direct object of the verb. In the Greek text, it appears before the verb.

but He used them only under the control of the Holy Spirit and within the will of the Father for His earthly life. There is no indication that He ever used any of the divine characteristics during his first thirty years of human existence. When the Spirit came upon Him at His baptism, He began to use these divine attributes.

2. He took a servant attitude

The self-emptying of Christ is further explained by the fact that He "took upon him the form of a servant" (*morphēn doulou labōn*). The noun "servant" (*doulou*) refers to a slave rather than to a hired domestic (*diakonos*). The participle (*labōn*), translated "took upon him," looks at the time when He emptied Himself, namely, His incarnation at the conception.

A contrast must be seen between Christ's eternal existence in the "form of God" and His decision to take the "form of a servant." As God, He was sovereign, deserving to be served, but He became a slave in order to serve. The active voice of the verb (*labōn*) reveals that He willingly took the role of slave; it was not forced upon Him. Jehovah called Him "my servant" (Isa. 42:1). Christ Himself said: "Lo, I come . . . to do thy will, O God" (Heb. 10:7).

Although there is an equality of persons within the divine essence, there is a voluntary subordination to carry out the redemptive purpose. He declared: "I seek not mine own will, but the will of the Father which hath sent me" (John 5:30). Within the oneness of a family, there is a personal equality of husband and wife, and yet there is a functional headship (I Cor. 11:3). In the same sense there is a functional headship of the Father over the Son.

A servant has no outward display of glory. As the preincarnate God, the glory of Christ radiated from His sovereign being (Isa. 6:1–5; John 12:41). That glory, when veiled within human flesh, manifested itself through servile acts of grace and truth (John 1:14). On one occasion though, He "was transfigured" (Matt. 17:2). Literally, he was "metamorphosed" (*metemorphōthē*). There was a change of "form" *(morphē)*. The glory of His divine person, which deserved to be served, thus shone through the flesh of His humanity in which He came to serve.

3. *He became human*

The sovereign Son of God inwardly "took the form of a servant," but outwardly He "was made in the likeness of men." The verb "made" *(genomenos)* again looks at the event of the incarnation—specifically at the conception, not the birth. The conception was supernatural, but the fetal development, the birth, and the physical-psychical growth (Luke 2:52) were all normal human experiences. John used the same verb in his declaration: "And the Word was made flesh *(egeneto)*, and dwelt among us" (John 1:14). Elsewhere, Paul used it twice: "But when the fulness of the time was come, God sent forth his Son, made *(genomenon)* of a woman, made under the law" (Gal. 4:4). The verb means to become what one presently is not. God the Son was an eternal spirit being, but He became a flesh and blood person.

The phrase "likeness of men" does not imply that He was less than a real man. The word "likeness" *(homoiōmati)* means that He appeared as real men appear. He walked and talked like ordinary men; He did not have a halo around His head nor did a glow emanate from His body. In their dealings with Christ, men treated Him as another man.

Jesus came "in the likeness of sinful flesh" (Rom. 8:13). He was a real man, yet he inherited no sin nature from His mother. A sin nature, however, is not an innate part of the human nature. Adam was a perfect man when God created him, yet he did not have a sinful tendency; he acquired it when he deliberately disobeyed God. Christ neither inherited nor obtained a sin nature; nevertheless, His humanity was just as perfect and complete as that of any man. He "knew no sin" (II Cor. 5:21), was tempted yet "without sin" (Heb. 4:15), "did no sin" (I Peter 2:22), and "in him is no sin" (I John 3:5). Only He could challenge His critics: "Which of you convinceth me of sin?" (John 8:46).

C. His Crucifixion (2:8)

This verse is built around one finite verb "(humbled")
supported by two participles ("being found" and "became").

1. He was treated as a man.

He was "found in fashion as a man." The word "fashion"
(schēmati) deals with external appearance. Men had a sense
perception of Him, but they did not see Him as He really
was. They saw a man, not the God-man. Divine illumination
is needed before one can properly identify Jesus Christ as
God incarnate (Matt. 11:25–27; 16:17).

Christ's enemies saw Him as a blaspheming man. If they
had known who He really was, they "would not have
crucified the Lord of glory" (I Cor. 2:8). His half-brothers
hurled sarcasms at Him (John 7:3–5). His hometown gave
Him no honor (Mark 6:1–6). Even Peter rebuked Him for His
death predictions (Matt. 16:22).

Men receive both their personality and their human nature
from their natural parents. God the Son was a divine person
with a divine nature who acquired a human nature. He did
not receive a personality from Mary. As a result of the incarnation, He was one person with two natures, divine and
human.[10]

2. He humbled Himself

Christ was not humbled by others, but rather, He "humbled himself" *(etapeinōsen heauton)*. It involved a voluntary
submission of His will to the directive will of the Father. In
the agony of Gethsemane, He concluded: "O my Father, if it
be possible, let this cup pass from me: nevertheless not as I
will, but as thou wilt" (Matt. 26:39).

Thereafter, He submitted Himself to the arrest, the trials,
and the mockeries. Even Pilate marvelled at Christ's quiet
acceptance of His predicament (Matt. 27:14). He was the sac-

---

[10]Theologians identify this truth as the hypostatic union.

rificial lamb of God, the fulfillment of messianic prophecy: "He was oppressed, and he was afflicted, yet he opened not his mouth: He is brought as a lamb to the slaughter, and as a sheep before her shearers is dumb, so he openeth not his mouth" (Isa. 53:7).

Christ thus possessed "lowliness of mind" (2:3). The word "lowliness" (*tapeinos*) comes from the verbal stem of "humbled" (*etapeinōsen*). He thus esteemed others better than Himself by His willingness to die for them (Rom. 5:6–8).

3. He became obedient to death

In his exposition of Christ's obedience, Paul stressed both the fact and the type of His death. *First,* its factuality is seen in the phrase: " ... became obedient unto death." Christ knew that His incarnation in a human body presupposed death in that same body (Heb. 10:5–10). His blood had to be shed to produce remission of sins (Heb. 9:22). One observed:

> Though he were a Son, yet learned he obedience by the things which he suffered;
> And being made perfect, he became the author of eternal salvation unto all them that obey him (Heb. 5:8–9).

Martin commented that "only a divine being can accept death as obedience; for ordinary men it is a necessity."[11]

Second, its type is "even the death of the cross." To the Jew, this was an accursed way to die (Deut. 21:23; Gal. 3:13). To the Roman, it was the execution of a criminal. No Roman citizen, including Paul, would have to die this shameful death. To the ordinary man, it was both painful and embarrassing.

The extent of the humiliation of Christ can be seen in His descent from being in the form of God to the lowest form of human death.

[11]Ralph P. Martin, *The Epistle of Paul to the Philippians,* p. 102.

III. THE EXALTATION OF CHRIST (2:9–11)

It seems paradoxical that in spiritual matters, the way up is the way down. Peter admonished: "Humble yourselves therefore under the mighty hand of God, that he may exalt you in due time (I Peter 5:6; cf. James 4:10). The conclusive connective "wherefore" *(dio)* thus joins these two aspects of Christ's life.

A. God Exalted Him (2:9a)

The exaltation of Christ was due to His total submission to the will of the Father, not just because He was God. Christ Himself said: "And whosoever shall exalt himself shall be abased; and he that shall humble himself shall be exalted" (Matt. 23:12; Luke 14:11; 18:14).

This verb "exalted," used only here in the New Testament and only of Christ, means to lift above or to lift beyond *(huperupsōse)*. The adverb "highly" *(huper)* is actually the preposition prefixed to the verb. This act of God fulfilled the prophecy of the suffering servant: "Behold, my servant shall deal prudently, he shall be exalted and extolled, and be very high" (Isa. 52:13).

The exaltation involved both the resurrection of Christ from the realm of Hades and His ascension into the very presence of the Father within the third heaven. Today, He is seated "on the right hand of the Majesty on high" (Heb. 1:3). No creature, whether man or angel, would ever dare to sit in God's holy presence, but Christ is there. Only God could ever sit beside God.

This exaltation involves supremacy over the natural creation because He is the divine creator and over the church because He is the divine-human redeemer (Col. 1:15–19). This exaltation made possible the sending forth of the Holy Spirit (Acts 2:33), intercession for believers (Rom. 8:34), headship over the church (Eph. 1:20–23), the conferral of spiritual gifts (Eph. 4:7–11), and representation before God (Heb. 4:14–16).

THE HUMILIATION AND EXALTATION OF CHRIST

B. God Gave Him a Name (2:9b–11)

Parents gave their children names which had special significance (Gen. 29:32–35). God revealed Himself through the names by which He described Himself (Gen. 17:1; Ex. 3:14). Pentecost explains: "Name is used here in its Old Testament sense where the name represents the total person. It bespeaks the office, the rank, and the dignity attached to the person because of his position.

The given name is "above every name." The term "above" *(huper)* is the same word translated as "highly" (2:9a). It thus is a name which denotes exalted supremacy.

1. Every knee will bow (2:10)

The bowing of the knee implies a sincere act of reverence, respect, and submission. Robertson wrote: "Not perfunctory genuflections, whenever the name of Jesus is mentioned, but universal acknowledgment of the majesty and power of Jesus who carries his human name and nature to heaven."[13]

This reverence has a threefold scope. *First,* the adoration "in heaven" comes from holy angels and redeemed men who have died (Eph. 1:21; Heb. 12:22–24; Rev. 4:9–11; 5:11–12). *Third,* the submission from "under the earth" comes from fallen angels and unregenerate men existing in Hades (Luke 16:19–31), Tartarus (II Peter 2:4), or the lake of fire (Matt. 25:41; Rev. 20:11–15).

2. Every tongue will confess

Both the content and the goal of the confession are set forth. *First,* the content is the name. The connective "that" *(hoti)* can be either explanatory or recitative. When explanatory, this translation is the result: " . . . that Jesus Christ is Lord." The predicate ("is") is not found in the Greek text, but is supplied to fit in with this usage of the connective. The

---

[12]J. Dwight Pentecost, *The Joy of Living,* p. 77.
[13]A. T. Robertson, *Word Pictures,* IV, p. 446.

word *hoti*, however, can be used to introduce a direct quotation; thus, the content of the confession is actually given: "Lord Jesus Christ" *(Kurios Jesous Christos)*. Every tongue will confess the deity, the humanity, and the redemptive office of the Savior. For some (holy angels and saved men), this confession represents their worship and praise, whereas for others (fallen angels and unsaved men) it designates their total submission to His absolute sovereignty.

Second, the goal of the confession, indicated by the preposition "to" *(eis),* is the "glory of God the Father" (cf. Eph. 1:6, 12, 14).

The time of the confession is not stated. It could occur at the beginning of the millennial reign of Christ (Rev. 5:8–14) or at the time of the Great White Throne Judgment when the old system passes away to make room for the new (Rev. 20:10–21:2).

Questions for Discussion

1. How can the mind of Christ be developed daily? What factors attempt to prevent this expression?

2. How can the deity of Christ be proved to a Jehovah's Witness? to a Jew?

3. How can believers empty themselves today? What are the marks of genuine humility?

4. What the characteristics of true servanthood? How can churches foster the spirit of service?

5. Are enough sermons preached on the hypostatic union, the truth that Christ is one person with two natures? Can Christians theologically express themselves in the right way?

6. Should modern worship include the bowing of the knee and the confession of the mouth?

7

The Marks of Humble Service
Philippians 2:12–16

Within Christianity, man plays both an active and a passive part. In salvation he must believe, and yet he must be quickened. In spiritual growth, it is imperative for him to walk in holiness, but it is also necessary for him to be led by the Spirit. Human accountability and divine sovereignty thus form two sides for the channel of redemptive purpose.

In this section Paul develops further his admonitions to the church (cf. 1:27–2:4). The illustration of Christ's humility only heightened their obligation to become true servants of the gospel. This portion is structured around two main commands ("work out" and "do").

I. EFFORT (2:12–13)

The resultant connective "wherefore" *(hōste)* shows the logical conclusion to the appeal to have the mind of Christ (2:5ff). True theology is always practical.

Genuine effort involves both man and God as colaborers. The believer cannot become spiritual by himself nor can Christ live His life through an unyielded vessel.

A. Human Responsibility (2:12)

The vocative "my beloved" reveals Paul's personal concern for the church. Earlier, he identified them as "brethren"

(1:12); later, he used the same description (3:1, 13, 17; 4:8). He joined the two titles in a subsequent emotional outburst (4:1). Thus, he regarded the membership of the church as genuine believers.

1. Obedience

Their obedience, like that of the Romans (Rom. 16:19), was known to all. They "always obeyed." The adverb "always" shows the stability of their Christian walk. The verb "obeyed" *(hupēkousate)* is a compound form of two words: "under" *(hupo)* and "hear" *(akouō)*. Thus, a person obeys when he puts himself under the authority of one who is speaking. The Philippians obeyed God, His word, Paul, and their church officers (1:1). Their obedience manifested Christ's obedience (2:8). They put into practice the concepts of true spiritual slavery:

> Know ye not, that to whom ye yield yourselves servants to obey, his servants ye are to whom ye obey; whether of sin unto death, or of obedience unto righteousness?
> But God be thanked, that ye were the servants of sin, but ye have obeyed from the heart that form of doctrine which was delivered you (Rom. 6:16–17).

2. Work

In the Greek text, the imperative ("work out") appears at the very end of the verse. Literally, it means: "Keep working down" *(katergazesthe)*. It involves a constant process of self-initiated activity.[1] Muller claims that the believer "must finish, must carry to conclusion, must apply to its fullest consequences what is already given by God in principle."[2] When a believer is thoroughly working at his spiritual development, he is working out what God is working in. He is

[1] Present middle imperative.
[2] Jac. J. Muller. *The Epistles of Paul to the Philippians and to Philemon,* p. 91.

putting his position into practice. Paul elsewhere wrote: "For we are his workmanship, created in Christ Jesus unto good works, which God hath before ordained that we should walk in them" (Eph. 2:10).

The preposition prefix *kata* intensifies the word *katergazesthe* and means that the work should be brought to a proper finish. Just as "tribulation worketh patience" (Rom. 5:3), so a believer should complete what God has started.

Three features of this work are set forth. *First, the time* of the work is seen in the phrase: " . . . not as in my presence only, but now much more in my absence." The negative "not" *(mē)* reveals that this time-expression must go with the imperative ("work out") rather than with the indicative verb ("obeyed").[3] The "presence" could refer either to the past during the apostle's first visit to their city or to his anticipated return (1:27; 2:24). He had observed their rapid spiritual growth, and he also was convinced that they would prosper under his future ministry. He knew, however, that their advancement could not be dependent upon his personal supervision of their lives. The strong contrast ("but now much more") manifests his concern that they must learn to mature without his personal help. They needed God to grow in grace and knowledge, but they did not need Paul (2:13).

Second, the object of the work is "your own salvation." A person cannot work *for* his salvation, but he can work *out* his spiritual position (Rom. 4:5; Eph. 2:8–10). Biblical salvation involves deliverance from the penalty of sin (II Tim. 1:9), from its power (Heb. 7:25), and from its presence (Rom. 13:11). The Philippians were saved people (1:6; 3:1); thus, the "salvation" *(sōtērian)* here refers to the daily struggle for victory over the sin nature. Each believer is responsible for his own ("your own") success or failure. He cannot achieve growth for others nor can he blame others for his carnality.

Third, the attitude of work is "with fear and trembling." When men perceive God as He is and what He wants to do

---

[3]The negative for the imperative mood is *mē,*, whereas it is *ou* for the indicative.

through their lives, these good emotional responses will be produced in them. They do not mean a psychological frailty nor a fear of hostile men and adverse circumstances. Paul preached with the two qualities of "fear and trembling" (I Cor. 2:3). The Corinthian revival was marked by them (II Cor. 7:15). Slaves were to obey their masters with fear and trembling (Eph. 6:5). Obedience and holy emotions are companions. Men must never forget that they are sinful creatures deserving God's worst. They should not take lightly the gracious gift of salvation.

B. Divine Responsibility (2:13)

The connective "for" *(gar)* gives the explanation for the preceding command. Man must work because God is working. Four aspects of this divine work are set forth in this verse.

1. Subject of the work

The Greek text reads: "For God is the one who is working in you.... "[4] The title "God" *(ho theos)* appears with the definite article *(ho);* thus, this is a direct reference to the Father (cf. 2:9). All persons of the Triune Being, however, are actively involved in the life of each believer. The Father is the husbandman who prunes and cleanses each saint (John 15:1–2). The Holy Spirit produces His fruit within the child of God (Gal. 5:22–23). Christ lives by faith through each Christian (Gal. 2:20).

The divine activity is literally an *in-working (ho energōn).* The literal transliteration of this participle is "the one who energizes." God's inner work deals with character, and man's outer work manifests his conduct.

---

[4] The word "God" is in the emphatic position at the beginning of the sentence.

2. *Location of the work*

God works within the human life ("in you"). This involves the total personality, including the intellect, the emotions, and the will. He does not want to be excluded from any area of human experience.

God is actively working within natural creation. He created it and He now sustains it (Col. 1:15–19). What men call natural law is really the normal work of the immanent God within His world. In the same manner, God is not content just to indwell the body of the believer, but He is energizing the new life which He has quickened.

3. *Purpose of the work*

The two infinitives "to will" and "to do," show the two purposes of the divine inworking. *First*, He desires "to will" *(to thelein)*. The will of God manifests His purpose. It includes that which He has unconditionally determined to do within the life of all believers regardless of their faithfulness. Paul thus wrote:

> And we know that all things work together for good to them that love God, to them who are the called according to his purpose.
>
> For whom he did foreknow, he also did predestinate to be conformed to the image of his Son, that he might be the firstborn among many brethren.
>
> Moreover whom he did predestinate, them he also called: and whom he called, them he also justified: and whom he justified, them he also glorified (Rom. 8:28–30).

It also includes that which He wants to do within each Christian; however, it is conditioned upon the believer's obedience and submission to His will (Rom. 12:1–2; I Thess. 4:3). God does not force spirituality upon anyone who refuses to have it, but He still continues to work out His purpose. Instead of blessing, He may bring chastisement upon a disobedient child (Heb. 12:5–11). The commands to repent and to be reconciled are constantly set forth before His erring saints. The present tense of the infinitive points to the daily will of God for each Christian.

Second, God desires "to do" *(to energein).* Without the prefix, this is the same verb as "worketh" *(energōn).* The energy of God manifests His power to accomplish His purpose. God never commands a believer to do something without Him supplying the ability to do it. The apostle later testified: "I can do all things through Christ which strengtheneth me" (4:13). Divine grace and sufficiency are always available for men to do the tasks appointed them (II Cor. 3:15). Paul admitted: "I labored more abundantly than they all: yet not I, but the grace of God which was with me" (I Cor. 15:10). Men, created and regenerated by God, are like electrical appliances; they can function only when they are plugged into the divine source of power.

4. *Goal of the work*

God works for His own glory ("of his good pleasure"). All aspects of salvation, including election, predestination, acceptance, redemption, forgiveness, illumination, and sealing, are executed for "the praise of the glory of his grace" (Eph. 1:6, 12, 14). They are decreed "according to the good pleasure of his will" (Eph. 1:5) and "according to his good pleasure which he hath purposed in himself" (Eph. 1:9). A believer must find pleasure in what God finds pleasure. When he does, then he will have joy and fulfillment. Then he will know the good, acceptable, perfect will of God (Rom. 12:1–2). Then he will experience the ultimate purpose of man: "Fear God, and keep his commandments: for this is the whole duty of man" (Eccl. 12:13).

II. LACK OF COMPLAINT (2:14–16)

The first command (vv. 12, 13) dealt with the believer's vertical relationship to God, whereas this second imperative concerns his horizontal relationships to situations and people. The first was to be obeyed with a positive attitude; the second is to be discharged without a negative outlook.

THE MARKS OF HUMBLE SERVICE

A. The Explanation of the Command (2:14)

1. The Action

Paul simply declared: "Do all things." The present imperative *(poieite)* stresses the necessity to keep on doing at all times and in all situations. At the marriage ceremony, the bride and groom promise to love each other in the midst of both good and bad times. Like Job, the believer must recognize that both good and evil will come into his life (Job 2:10). He must persevere in holiness and dedication. He must forever be a doer of the Word of God (James 1:22).

All believers are the objects of divine "workmanship" *(poiēma;* Eph. 2:10). That noun comes from the same stem as this imperative *(poieō).* Christians must do as God is doing.

The direct object "all things" is in the emphatic position, appearing at the very beginning of the sentence. It could thus be translated: "All things keep on doing." The phrase includes all that God has commanded. Love for God manifests itself in the keeping of His directives (I John 5:2). The Christian should not resist this sovereign authority over his life because "His commandments are not grievous" (I John 5:2). Life outside of the will of God is heavy and burdensome, but willing conformity brings rest to the soul (Matt. 11:28–30).

2. The attitude

Christians are to avoid "murmurings and disputings." When adversity comes, natural man has the tendency to blame God or other people for his difficulties. He refuses to fault himself or to rejoice in tribulation. The classic example of this human weakness occurred after the first sin was committed in the Garden of Eden. Adam blamed God for giving Eve to him, and Eve subsequently pointed an accusing finger at the serpent (Gen. 3:11–13).

First, the noun "murmurings" *(goggusmōn)* comes from a verb which means to mutter or to grumble. J. D. Pentecost defines it as an "outward expression of an inner lawlessness and rebellion that shakes the fist in the face of God and re-

109

pudiates His right to rule, that questions His love and His wisdom."[5] When the children of Israel came out of Egypt, they immediately began to murmur. They complained at the Red Sea when the chariots of the Egyptians threatened to overtake them (Exod. 14:10–12), at Marah where the waters were bitter (Exod. 15:24), in the wilderness of Sin when they had no food (Exod. 16:3), at Rephidim where they had no water (Exod. 17:3), and at Kadesh-Barnea because the spies reported the presence of giants in the land (Num. 14:2). Although the derision was directed toward the human leaders, Moses clarified their dissatisfaction: "Your murmurings are not against us, but against the Lord" (Exod. 16:9). Very seldom would a believer aim his complaint directly at God; rather, he points it in a subtle fashion at the divinely appointed leaders (cf. Acts 6:1). Since men are fallible, he can influence others to agree with his criticism of his predicament.

Second, the noun "disputings" *(dialogismōn)* comes from a verb which conveys the idea of dialogue or argument. Pentecost defines it as "an inward intellectual rebellion where the mind weighs the truth of God, sits in judgment upon it, and condemns it."[6] It emphasizes mental complaint, whereas murmurings reflect an emotional response.

Both attitudes, of course, reveal a spirit of carnality. They constitute rebellion against what God wants men to do, when He wants them to do it, where it should be done, and why it should occur. In essence, they are like the clay which questions the potter as he fashions it (Rom. 9:19–21). Such constant bickering will lead to divine chastisement. Contemporary believers should benefit from the past failures of the Israelites (I Cor. 10:1–5). As Paul wrote: "Neither murmur ye, as some of them also murmured, and were destroyed of the destroyer" (I Cor. 10:10).

[5]J. Dwight Pentecost, *The Joy of Living,* p. 94.
[6]Ibid.

B. The Purposes of the Command (2:15–16a)

The connective "that" *(hina)* shows the purpose for the fulfillment of the command.[7] There is always a holy reason behind a divine command. The verb "ye may be" should be translated "that you might become" *(genēsthe)*. There is a difference between being a Christian and living the Christian life. The former refers to position, but the latter to practice. The Philippians, who were saints (1:1), needed to become more saintly in their human relationships. Four purposes are expressed here.

1. Blameless behavior

It is difficult to develop a firm distinction between the two adjectives. Perhaps a person may be "blameless" in what he says or does and "harmless" in what he is.

First, the concept "blameless" *(amemptoi)* means a freedom from censure. In his unsaved Pharasaical life, Paul regarded himself as blameless concerning the righteous demands of the law (3:6). In his apostolic ministry, he behaved unblamably among the churches (I Thess. 2:10). For Christians, he prayed that their "whole spirit and soul and body be preserved blameless unto the coming of our Lord Jesus Christ" (I Thess. 5:23). To be blameless means to be judged by others to be innocent and pure.

Second, the meaning of "harmless" *(akeraioi)* is to be unmixed or unadulterated.[8] It was used of solid gold jewelry which was without any alloy. In medicine, it referred to a prescription which was useful but harmless. Paul wanted believers to be "simple (same word) concerning evil" (Rom. 16:19). Such purity is only attained by the heat of testing through adversity.

---

[7]It is a purpose *(hina)* clause, normally introduced as *"in order that."*
[8]It comes from the verb *kerannumi* (to mix).

2. *Spotless children*

Three descriptions of their desired position are given here. *First,* they were to be literally "children of God." The Greek text reads "children" *(tekna)* rather than "sons" *(huioi).* A sinner becomes a child of God by regeneration (John 1:12), but he is put into the position of a son by adoption (Gal. 4:4–7). As children, they inherited the divine nature of their heavenly Father. The absence of the definite article *(tekna theou)* shows that they possessed this nature and that they were not the only ones to be in the family of God.

Second, he wanted them to become children "without rebuke." This negative adjective literally means "without spot or blemish" *(amōmēta).* A believer has been washed of the guilt and filth of his sin so that he is clean in God's sight (John 13:10; I Cor. 6:11); however, he must still be cleansed from the daily defilement of the world (John 13:10; I John 1:9). Ultimately, it will require the return of Christ to produce total sanctification (Eph. 5:26–27).

Third, their environment was not conducive to holiness because they lived "in the midst of a crooked and perverse nation." It will be easy to be a spotless child in the holy city, but it is most difficult to be clean in the midst of moral filth. The word "crooked" *(skolias)* implies that which is curved in contrast to that which is straight. It marked both Israel and the pagan nations as they embraced spiritual and physical adultery (Deut. 32:5; Ps. 78:8; Acts 2:40). The adjective "perverse" *(diestrammenēs)* denotes that which is permanently distorted and twisted.[9] The world of ungodly men will never be totally reformed or regenerated; rather, their immoral influence will increase (II Tim. 3:1–7). No believer should expect to convert the world nor should he permit the world to change him.

---

[9]It is a perfect passive participle.

3. Lights to the world

Christians should be marked by separation from the world, not by isolation from it. They must "shine as lights in the world." Christ shone in the world of spiritual darkness (John 1:4). He sat with sinners, but He was still separate from them. He testified: "As long as I am in the world, I am the light of the world" (John 9:5). After He informed His disciples that they were the light of the world, He charged them: "Let your light so shine before men, that they may see your good works, and glorify your Father which is in heaven" (Matt. 5:14, 16). Light must function where it is needed, namely, in the darkness. Paul reminded all Christians: "For ye were sometimes darkness, but now are ye light in the Lord: walk as children of light" (Eph. 5:8). Again, they must manifest their position, which reflects the nature of God, by their practice. God is light and He enlightens, and so should His children (I John 1:5).

4. Word bearers

Believers must be diligent in "holding forth the word of life." The verb *epechontes* means not just to hold fast to one-self, but also to hold forth to others. A person can only witness to that which he already possesses. It also conveys the idea of giving one's attention to something. In this sense, the lame man "gave heed" (same word) to the instructions of Peter and John (Acts 5:5).

Jesus Christ is *the* Word of Life (I John 1:1); however, each portion of Scripture is *a* word of life about Him. The written Word reveals the living Word to those who are dead in spiritual darkness.

C. The Results of the Command (2:16b)

The word "that" *(eis)* shows the results which would occur within the life of Paul if the Philippians would obey his two commands.

STAND UNITED IN JOY

1. Boastful rejoicing

Paul knew that he would appear "in the day of Christ." This event includes both the return of the Savior and His subsequent judgment of believers. It involves the reunion of the saints with each other and with the Lord (II Thess. 2:1).

In that day, Paul wanted to "rejoice" over what his ministry had accomplished in the lives of the Philippians. The word "rejoicing" *(kauchēma)* includes a pride of achievement and should not be limited to mere joy (cf. 4:4; *chairete*).[10] There is joy when a sinner receives salvation, but there is greater joy when spiritual children walk in truth (III John 4). The apostle could honestly confess about all of his converts: "For what is our hope, or joy, or crown of rejoicing? Are not even ye in the presence of our Lord Jesus Christ at his coming? For ye are our glory and joy" (I Thess. 2:19–20). The joy of parenthood can easily be lessened by the disobedience of the children (Heb. 13:17).

2. Productive labor

Paul was not content with merely a good start. He wanted his spiritual children to go on to maturity and holiness. He wanted them to be right, both in position and practice. He determined the success of his ministry by two concepts.

First, he did not want the judgment seat of Christ to manifest the possibility that he had "run in vain." This would occur if he had preached a faulty or a partial message (Gal. 2:2). It would happen if he had taught with carnal motivations or immoral behavior (I Cor. 9:26). Paul would have been disappointed if he had been surrounded by divisive, immature converts.

Second, he did not want the future to manifest that he had "labored in vain." Both legalism and Satan could cause this result (Gal. 4:11; I Thess. 3:15).

His race and labor were correct. He knew that God would reward his integrity and faithfulness to the work. No genuine

---

[10]The phrase "I may rejoice" is not a verb but a noun.

labor is in vain in the Lord (I Cor. 15:58). Even the Messiah was frustrated in His ministry to Israel: "I have labored in vain, I have spent my strength for nought, and in vain: yet surely my judgment is with the Lord, and my work with my God" (Isa. 49:4). All Christian workers have wondered about the value of their work in other's lives, especially when the people persistently refuse to follow their leadership. They must, however, finish their course with joy and expectation (Acts 20:24; II Tim. 4:7).

Questions for Discussion

1. Do Christian leaders love their people as they should? Do they express it in their words and actions?

2. Do Christians fear God today? If not, what can be done to produce genuine reverence?

3. When do the human and the divine conflict? When do they harmonize?

4. Why do believers often complain? Cite some illustrations where they may murmur when the unsaved do not.

5. What are the characteristics of a crooked people? In what ways does our country manifest these?

6. How can believers be more effective in their witness?

7. Why do Christian workers often get discouraged? How can they be helped?

8

The Three Examples of Humility
Philippians 2:17–30

Theory must be put into practice and ideas must be dressed in flesh. Learners want to be shown as well as to be told. The apostle thus cited as examples three men who manifested the mind of Christ and who were working out without complaint what God was working in. All three exhibited the joy of unity, humility, and concern for others. They were Paul himself, Timothy, and Epaphroditus.

I. PAUL (2:17–18)

Paul was not afraid to point men to himself nor to list himself as the first example (cf. 4:9). Men must be, know, and do all that God expects before they can require commitments from others. A good teacher, leader, or parent should be able to ask others to observe him as well as to listen to him (Ezra 7:10).

A. His Offering (2:17a)

1. In the past

The prepositional phrase ("upon the sacrifice and service of your faith") points to that time when the apostle completely surrendered his life to God. All believers should "present [their] bodies a living sacrifice, holy, acceptable unto God, which is [their] reasonable service" (Rom. 12:1–2).

This nonrepeatable decision[1] could occur at conversion, but it is usually made in a postregeneration experience. Unfortunately, many believers never make this commitment to lose their lives for Christ's sake (Matt. 16:24–25).

The "sacrifice" *(thusiāi)* refers to the Jewish rite of the burnt offering where an animal was totally consumed upon the altar to show the complete and voluntary dedication of oneself to God. The offerer made this sacrifice because he was thankful for all that God had done for him. These "mercies of God" provided the incentive (Rom. 12:1). Elsewhere, the apostle wrote:

> For the love of Christ constraineth us; because we thus judge, that if one died for all, then were all dead:
> And that he died for all, that they which live should not henceforth live unto themselves, but unto him which died for them, and rose again (II Cor. 5:14–15).

Thus, Paul gave his life entirely over to God to live for His glory (1:20).

A commitment to God also brings a commitment to others. Paul knew that his service to God would involve service to man ("and service of your faith"). The term "service" *(leitourgiāi)* transliterates as "liturgy;" thus, helping others is actually a religious ministry. The apostle served them by declaring how they could have saving faith and by encouraging them to grow in faith.

2. In the future

The conditional clause ("if I be offered") reveals the strong possibility of imminent martyrdom for the apostle.[2] Paul had given his life to live for God and others; now he was willing

---

[1]The verb "present" *(paratēsai)* is an aorist active infinitive.

[2]Indicated by "if" *(ei)* with the present tense. The verb *(spendomai)* was used of the additional drink offering which was poured out upon the burnt offering (Exod. 29:38–41; Lev. 23:12–13; Num. 15:1–10). Paul had given his life.

to give his life to die for them. In this way he emulated the self-emptying of Christ and His obedience unto death (2:7–8). On his way to Jerusalem where he was subsequently imprisoned, he testified that he was ready to die for Christ (Acts 21:13). Just before his actual martyrdom during his second Roman imprisonment, Paul confidently asserted that he was "now ready to be offered" (II Tim. 4:6; same word).[3]

Even those who had been saved from a pagan background would have understood this figure of speech. They were acquainted with the libation of wine or perfume poured out in the concluding rites of a sacrifice to a polytheistic deity.

B. His Rejoicing (2:17b–18)

Rejoicing needs to be reciprocal; it must have two directions. *First,* Paul said: "I joy, and rejoice with you all." He rejoiced in the prospect of a death which would glorify God and which would advance their faith. *Second,* he called upon them to rejoice with him ("do ye joy and rejoice with me").[4] They were saddened by Paul's imprisonment, but he wanted their despair to be turned into joy by the truth of his epistle and by the personal witness of Timothy and Epaphroditus.

II. TIMOTHY (2:19–24)

Timothy assisted Paul in the original evangelization of the city. The apostle identified the young associate as a cosender of the epistle (1:1). Now he is mentioned as a second example of unity, humility, and altruism.

A. His Purpose for Timothy (2:19, 23–24)

Paul aways made his travel plans in total submission to the will of God. His human desire is seen in the verb "I trust"

---

[3]This word is used only twice in the New Testament, both times concerning Paul.

[4]The first set of two verbs are indicative, but the second set could be imperative instead of indicative.

(literally, "I hope," *elpizō*). His acknowledgement of the divine will is evident in the prepositional phrase ("in the Lord Jesus"). At the end of his second missionary journey, he announced to the residents of Ephesus after his brief contact with them: "I will return again unto you, if God will" (Acts 18:21). He promised the Roman Christians that he would come to them "with joy by the will of God" (Rom. 15:32). He personified the biblical injunction: "For that ye ought to say, If the Lord will, we shall live, and do this, or that" (James 4:15).

At the beginning and the end of this section, he presented three purposes concerning Timothy. In between, he discussed the character qualifications of his young associate.

1. To send him to the church (2:19a, 23)

Paul hoped "to send Timothy shortly" unto the church. The adverb *(tacheōs)* conveys the idea of imminent quickness (cf. Rev. 1:1).[5] Later, Paul used the adverb "presently" *(exautēs)*.

The fact of sending was sure; only the time of sending was indefinite. The latter is clarified in the conditional statement: " ... so soon as I shall see how it will go with me" (v. 23). The closing words literally read "the things concerning me" *(ta peri eme)*. He was awaiting the disposition of his appeal and trial before Caesar and the Roman authorities. He fully expected that it would be favorable and that it would be given at any moment.

Although the apostle needed Timothy in Rome, he was more concerned about the spiritual needs of the Philippians (cf. 2:4); thus he planned to give up one who belonged to him. This attitude reflected the mind of Christ who gave up what was His to reach others.

2. To be comforted (2:19b)

The conjunction "that" *(hina)* shows the second purpose: " ... that I also may be of good comfort, when I know your

[5]The English word *tachometer* is based upon this adverb.

state." The connective "also" *(kai)* shows that Timothy would be the first to be cheered by the response of the church to the epistle which would have arrived before the associate. Then Timothy planned to report back to Paul, either by personal visit, letter, or a representative.

The verb here translated "I ... may be of good comfort" literally reads "I may have a good soul" *(eupsuchō)*. To have unity, or an effort of joint souls (1:27; 2:2), those souls must be spiritually healthy and pure. This condition, however, must be based upon knowledge. The adverb "when" indicates the time when Paul expected to be cheered.[6] It would happen when he received the report about the spiritual condition of the church ("your state").

3. *To prepare for the visit of the apostle (2:24)*

Paul then expressed confidence "in the Lord" that he himself would be able to visit Philippi. The verb ("I trust," *pepoitha*) is different than the one used for the sending of Timothy (2:19; *elpizō*). It denotes a settled assurance and conviction of heart produced by the indwelling God.[7] Both the intensive pronoun "myself" and the adverb "shortly" reinforce that inner persuasion. Such news, of course, would bring joy to the hearts of the Philippians and would stimulate them to obey the directives of the epistle.

B. His Preference for Timothy (2:20–22)

Why did Paul decide to send Timothy? Why not one of his other coworkers (cf. Philem. 24)? The apostle saw in Timothy some special qualities which the Philippians needed to develop.

---

[6]This phrase is actually introduced by the temporal aorist participle *gnous*.

[7]It is related to the word translated as "confidence" (1:25).

THE THREE EXAMPLES OF HUMILITY

1. He was like-minded (2:20a)

The term "like-minded" *(isopsuchon)* literally means "equal soul." Just as Jesus Christ was equal to the Father in deity (2:6), so Timothy was equal to Paul in the characteristics of unity, humility, and concern for others. This is a stronger and slightly different term than that used in the apostle's appeal to the church members (2:2; *sumpsuchoi*). Both Paul and Timothy shared the mind of Christ, thought the same things, and had the same spiritual goals.

The conjunction "for" *(gar)* gives the explanation for the choice of Timothy. The negative declaration ("I have no man") is striking in that Paul was surrounded at this time with men like Tychichus, Aristarchus, Mark, Epaphras, Demas, and Luke (Col. 4:7–14; Philem. 23–24).

2. He had concern (2:20b)

Three concepts are described here. *First,* Timothy was a caring person. The verb "will care" can be used of a self-destructive worry which profits no one (4:6; Matt. 6:25). Some people are so concerned about what others will think about them or do to them that they have no energy left to help those who have real needs. Timothy, however, manifested that same care for the churches which Paul possessed (II Cor. 11:28). He prayed, taught, and counseled others.

Second, Timothy's concern was genuine. The adverb "naturally" *(gnēsiōs)* normally is translated as "genuinely" or "truly." Later, Paul called him "my genuine child in the faith" (I Tim. 1:2; *gnēsiōi*). He was legitimate, not spurious, in his spiritual birth and development. He manifested the same nature as his spiritual father.

Third, Timothy had concern for the church ("for your state"). The phrase can be translated "the things concerning you" *(ta peri humōn)*. Since he was included in the opening greeting, he shared the apostle's concern over the spiritual weaknesses of the believers. He wanted to be the human instrument by which God would remedy the situation.

3. He was not selfish (2:21a)

Paul then pronounced a general indictment upon the motivation of gospel preachers (cf. 1:15–16). The words have a ring of sadness to them: "For all seek their own." Again, the connective "for" gives another reason for the sending of Timothy. Selfishness, a trait of sinful humanity, unfortunately permeates the Christian world as well. The possessive phrase can be translated "the things of themselves" (ta heautōn). The present tense of the verb shows that self-seeking will always be found in all segments of society.

The exclusion of Timothy from this group shows that he was not selfish. He was not in the ministry for what he could get out of it. He was a giver, not a taker. When Paul originally chose Timothy to accompany him, the associate was "well reported of by the brethren" (Acts 16:2). That virtue had not become tarnished by his close affiliation with the greatest of the apostles.

4. He manifested Christ (2:21b)

Selfish persons do not seek "the things which are Jesus Christ's." These "things" include the mind of Christ as seen in humility, obedience, and concern for others. Christ emptied Himself, Paul was willing to pour out himself, and Timothy was determined to seek the glorification of the Savior in his ministry to the church. As an equal soul to Paul, he could join him in saying, "For me to live is Christ" (1:21).

5. He was a servant (2:22)

In the salutation, both Paul and Timothy were introduced as "the servants of Jesus Christ" (1:1). Christ Himself took "the form of a servant" (2:7). The mind of Christ thus reveals an attitude of service. This quality could be seen in Timothy in three ways.

First, he was a proved servant. The Philippians were aware of his humility ("ye know"). They had contact with him on at least four occasions. He was in their midst when the church was started (Acts 16:12–40), when Paul sent him from Athens to Thessalonica (Acts 18:5; I Thess. 3:1–2), and twice during the third missionary journey (Acts 19:22; 20:3–6). They had empirical "proof" *(dokimēn)* that Timothy was a faithful worker. The word "proof" was used of the testing of precious metals through the heat of the fire (cf. I Peter 1:7). Church leaders, like deacons, should be proved so that people will have confidence in their leadership (I Tim. 3:10).

Second, he was a cooperative servant. Said Paul, " . . . he hath served with me." Some servants can work effectively when they labor alone but cannot get along with others when they have to serve in a team effort. Timothy, however, served "as a son with the father." Timothy was Paul's son in the faith and thus inherited the servant nature of the apostle (I Cor. 4:17; I Tim. 1:2; II Tim. 1:2). There was no competition between the two nor did Timothy seek to displace Paul. The prepositional phrase "with me" shows that Timothy served *with* Paul, not that he served the apostle directly; rather, they both served the Savior.

Third, he was a gospel servant. They both "served" *(edouleusen).*[8] He was "in the gospel" ministry in that he determined to further the outreach and the influence of the gospel message in the lives of both sinners and believers.[9] Both Paul and he were "striving together for the faith of the gospel" (1:27). This dedication reflected Christ's willing obedience to lay the foundation of the gospel through His death and resurrection (2:5–8).

III. EPAPHRODITUS (2:25–30)

Epaphroditus should not be confused with Epaphras, who was a member of the church at Colosse (Col. 1:7; 4:12). The name "Epaphroditus" means "lovely" or "charming." It is probably based upon Aphrodite, the pagan goddess of love

[8]The verb is related to the noun *(doulos).*

[9]The word "in" is the purpose preposition *eis,* normally given as "unto" (1:12).

and beauty. His name occurs only twice in the Scriptures, both times in this book (2:25; 4:18). The church had sent Epaphroditus to Rome to give Paul some money (4:18), and now the apostle planned to send him back home with the epistle.

A. His Character (2:25)

The verbs indicate that Paul sent Epaphroditus at the same time he dispatched the letter.[10] He deemed it "necessary" because his epistle was finished, Epaphroditus was well enough to travel, and he was concerned over their apprehension. In his identification of this outstanding Christian, Paul listed five positive characteristics:

1. Brother

Relationship is more crucial than responsibility; thus Paul first identified Epaphroditus as his "brother." They were both in the family of God through regeneration. They were also joined together with the brethren who resided in Philippi (1:12; 3:1). The usage of this term may indicate that Epaphroditus was not a direct convert of Paul's ministry as Timothy was.[11]

2. Worker

He is called a "companion in labor" (sunergon). They were both working out what God was working in. Paul never permitted his apostolic status to foster a superior spirit within himself. Rather, he saw himself as a coworker with God and with other believers in a common effort to reach men with the gospel.

---

[10]They are epistolary aorists, viewing the action from the standpoint of the readers. When the church read the letter, Epaphroditus had already been sent.

[11]Note the distinction in the two between "son" and "brother."

3. Soldier

He is also described as a "fellow soldier." He had put on the armor of God to war against sin and the devil (Eph. 6:10–17). He endured hardness as a good soldier of Jesus Christ (II Tim. 2:3). He doubtless fulfilled this qualification: "No man that warreth entangleth himself with the affairs of this life: that he may please him who hath chosen him to be a soldier" (II Tim. 2:4). He took his stand with Paul in an aggressive defense of the gospel (1:7).

4. Messenger

Epaphroditus had the above-mentioned three relationships with Paul; with the church (note "your") he had the following two. He was their "messenger" *(apostolon)*. This term is normally translated as "apostle," but he was not an apostle in the technical sense. Only those who saw the resurrected Christ and who were commissioned directly by Him to preach the gospel were regarded as the authoritative apostles (I Cor. 9:1–5; 15:7–9). In a general sense, however, he was sent by the church to Rome with a commission to carry out. Others were also called messengers or apostles in this nontechnical way (II Cor. 8:23). Epaphroditus was an apostle of the church ("your"), but not of Christ (Eph. 1:1).

5. Minister

He was also a minister to the needs of the apostle. The phrase ("he that ministered") is actually a noun *(leitourgon)*. It is used of official and sacred service. In this context it is also used of the service of both Paul and the church (2:17, 30). The gift of money sent by the church was a sacrifice to God, offered as a priestly function of believers (4:18). Just as Paul was willing to live and die in order that he might serve the faith of the Philippians, so Epaphroditus came close to death in his service to Paul. This action was a clear example of pure servanthood.

B. His Concern (2:26–28)

Epaphroditus truly looked on the things of others, not on his own things (2:4). This fact is clearly demonstrated in the details surrounding his sickness.

1. His compassion (2:26)

Two inner emotions are described here. *First*, he "longed after" his home church. The verbal construction emphasizes a prolonged duration of intense desire. It literally translates: "he was constantly longing after" *(epipothōn ēn)*.[12] This desire was of the same type that Paul expressed to the church (1:8). *Second*, he "was full of heaviness."[13] This is the same term used of Christ's agony in Gethsemane (Matt. 26:37; Mark 14:33). It stresses mental, emotional, and spiritual anguish.

The reason for these two emotional concerns is seen in the causal clause ("because that ye had heard that he had been sick"). In his labor at Rome, Epaphroditus became deathly ill. Word of this sickness somehow got back to the church at Philippi. Subsequently, he became informed that the church knew about his physical weakness. He then became concerned over their concern for him! He was the proverbial hospital patient worrying about the folks back home.

2. His healing (2:27)

The church knew that their member had become ill, but they apparently did not know the severity of his weakness. Paul now informed them that Epaphroditus "was sick nigh unto death." There is no indication what the nature of the sickness was.

The statement that "God had mercy on him" reveals the fact that God graciously healed him (cf. Mark 5:19). The de-

---

[12]It is a periphrastic imperfect construction, the usage of the present participle with the imperfect indicative of *eimi* ("to be").

[13]This verb is also a periphrastic imperfect. Both participles *(epipthōn* and *ademonōn)* use the same imperfect *ēn*).

terioration of Epaphroditus's health to this critical point shows that Paul was no longer performing miracles of healing to authenticate his apostleship. There is no indication in this verse that Paul laid hands on Epaphroditus and conferred healing upon him. Later, the apostle instructed Timothy to use wine for his many internal infirmities (I Tim. 5:23) and left Trophimus sick at Miletus (II Tim. 4:20).

God extended physical mercy to Epaphroditus and psychological mercy to Paul ("and not on him only, but on me also"). The healing was done for both of their benefits, but mainly for the emotional relief of the apostle. The negative purpose clause shows the real explanation behind the healing ("lest I should have sorrow upon sorrow"). The first sorrow came when the coworker became sick; the second sorrow would have come if Epaphroditus had died. Paul experienced the first sorrow and some apprehension about the second.

3. His reunion (2:28)

As soon as Epaphroditus was healed, Paul sent him in haste to the church. The adverb here translated "more carefully" (spoudaioterōs) connotes speed rather than caution.

The appearance of Epaphroditus at Philippi doubtless caused both surprise and joy because the church thought that he was still ill in Rome. They had not heard about his miraculous recovery.[14]

His return would accomplish two good results (note usage of "that"). *First,* the church would "rejoice" at his coming. *Second,* Paul would be "the less sorrowful" in that the anxious concern of all parties would have been turned into joy.

C. His Commendation (2:29)

1. Receive him

The conjunction "therefore" (oun) shows what response

---

[14]This is why Paul explained the background for the healing.

the Philippians should have toward Epaphroditus in the light of his dedicated service and return. The two imperatives give the two positive reactions. They first should "receive him in the Lord with all gladness." A spiritual reception involves these principles given by Christ:

> He that receiveth you receiveth me, and he that receiveth me receiveth him that sent me.
>
> He that receiveth a prophet in the name of a prophet shall receive a prophet's reward; and he that receiveth a righteous man in the name of a righteous man shall receive a righteous man's reward (Matt. 10:40–41).

2. Honor him.

They should "hold such in reputation." The word "such" *(tous toioutous)* is in the plural; therefore they were to esteem highly all men who were like Epaphroditus. The expression "in reputation" *(entimous)* literally means "in honor." The word is used of a precious, prized possession and of money (I Tim. 5:17). The adjective is used of Christ as the "precious" cornerstone of salvation (I Peter 2:4, 6). Humble servants of the Lord, like Epaphroditus, must be appreciated, and such appreciation should be given publicly.

D. His Commitment (2:30)

The reasons for Paul's commendation of Epaphroditus are introduced by the casual conjunction "because" *(hoti)*. Three reasons are listed.

1. He worked for Christ.

His motivation was "the work of Christ." He preached the gospel of Christ's death and resurrection. Paul once said of Timothy: " . . . he worketh the work of the Lord, as I also do" (I Cor. 16:10). This simple praise could now be spoken of Epaphroditus.

In addition, his labor made him "nigh unto death." Just as Christ in His obedience went into the death of the cross (2:8), so the Philippian messenger followed his Savior to the very threshold of physical death.

2. He did not regard his life.

The participle "regarding" *(parabouleusamenos)* was used of people who exposed themselves to danger. The thought is that Epaphroditus risked his life. A similar term, "riskers," *(parabolani)* was later applied to Christians who risked their lives for others.[15] In his concern for the needs of Paul, Epaphroditus did not look "on his own things," namely, the progressive weakness of his body (cf. 2:4).

3. He offered substitute service.

Epaphroditus was aware that the gift of the Philippians was not enough to meet the needs of the apostle; thus he worked to earn money. The more he worked, the weaker he grew. He tried to make up the difference ("to supply") between the actual amount of the gift and the needed total. The "lack" was not created by a deliberate attempt to withhold funds, because the church was later applauded for its generosity (4:10–19). Just as Christ died as the sin substitute for the needs of all men, so Epaphroditus almost died as the financial substitute for the Philippians.

---

[15]A. T. Robertson, *Word Pictures,* IV, p. 450.

STAND UNITED IN JOY

Questions for Discussion

1. What does it mean to offer one's self as a living sacrifice to God? How many Christians have done this? Have you?

2. What motivates a person to die for a cause? What prevents him from doing so?

3. In what ways do Christians make plans without consulting God? How can human and divine plans be harmonized?

4. In what ways do Christians manifest personal ambition and greed in the work of the Lord? How are they encouraged in this unwholesome pursuit?

5. Is it wise for members of the same family to work together in the same Christian effort? Are there advantages? Disadvantages?

6. Does God perform works of healing today? Are there genuine faith healers today?

9

The Danger of Legalism
Philippians 3:1–6

In the third chapter of this epistle, Paul discussed the threefold aspect of salvation against the background of doctrinal error. The exposition of this basic truth centered around three verbal concepts. *First,* Paul wanted to be "found in him"; that is justification (3:9). *Second,* his ambition was to "know him"; that is sanctification (3:10). *Third,* he desired to "look for him"; that is glorification (3:20). These three theological verities deal with the past, present, and future experiences of all believers—not just the apostle.

In this treatment of the doctrine of justification,[1] Paul had to distinguish between salvation by works through human effort and salvation by grace through faith. In this section, two major contrasts between Paul and the false teachers are set forth.

I. IN CIRCUMCISION (3:1–3)

The adverb "finally" *(to loipon)* does not signal the end of the epistle; rather, it designates an abrupt change in subject matter. Paul often used this device to introduce issues that needed to be discussed (cf. 4:8; I Thess. 4:1; II Thess. 3:1). This transitional thought translates: "As far as the rest is con-

---

[1] Justification is that act of God whereby He declares righteous that sinner who has been made righteous through faith in Christ.

cerned."[2] The vocative ("my brethren") also helps to make the switch of topic.

A. Necessity of Warning (3:1)

The opening command sets the tone for the entire chapter ("rejoice in the Lord"). They were not to rejoice, however, in who they were and what they had done. They were to rejoice constantly in all that Jesus Christ is and in all that He has graciously provided through His redemptive death and resurrection.[3] Such holy joy, however, can be threatened by the onslaught of doctrinal and moral error.

1. For Paul

A faithful preacher must not only declare truth, but also expose error. He must build and protect at the same time. When Nehemiah rebuilt the walls of Jerusalem, he followed this procedure: "For the builders, every one had his sword girded by his side, and so builded. And he that sounded the trumpet was by me" (Neh. 4:18).

Paul knew that he had "to write the same things" which he had taught them during his past visits to their city (cf. 3:18). Repetition and reinforcement are basic laws of pedagogy, the science of teaching. Peter likewise said to his readers: "Wherefore I will not be negligent to put you always in remembrance of these things, though ye know them, and be established in the present truth" (II Peter 1:12).

Such warnings were "not grievous" *(oknēron)* to Paul. It was not an irksome task. This adjective comes from a verb which means to delay or to hesitate *(okneō);* thus the apostle did not shrink from his responsibility to point out error. He informed the Ephesian elders that he was free from the blood of all men because he had declared "all the counsel of God"

---

[2]The construction uses an article with an adjective used as a substantive.

[3]The present imperative *(chairete)* stresses the continuous action of rejoicing.

(Acts 20:26–27). That declaration was further explained in these words:

> For I know this, that after my departing shall grievous wolves enter in among you, not sparing the flock.
> Also of your own selves shall men arise, speaking perverse things, to draw away disciples after them.
> Therefore watch, and remember, that by the space of three years I ceased not to warn every one night and day with tears (Acts 20:29–31).

2. For the church

The contrast between the two relationships to the warning is seen in the two connectives: "indeed ... but" *(men ... de).* It was "safe" for the Philippians. This adjective comes from a verb *(asphallō)* which means not to totter or to reel. The European scholar, Greijdanus, observed: "Repeated warning can prevent our losing sight of the danger and rouses us to continuous watchfulness.... It prevents negligence and thus promotes safety."[4]

B. Nature of Warning (2:2)

The same imperative ("beware") is repeated three times. This verb simply means to keep looking out, to continue watching, or to persist in seeing *(blepete).*[5]

Some have concluded that Paul was talking about three different groups: Gentiles, greedy teachers, and Jews. It seems better, however, to see the descriptions as three characteristics of the same group. They doubtlessly were the Judaizers who taught that a Gentile had to be circumcised in order to be saved (Acts 15:1). They should not be equated with the preachers who spoke the truth with faulty motivations (1:14–18).

---

[4]Cited by Jac. J. Muller, *The Epistles of Paul to the Philippians and to Philemon,* p. 105.

[5]**Present active imperative.**

STAND UNITED IN JOY

1. Beware of dogs

This warning depicts their *character*. The title "dogs" *(kunas)* is applied to the unsaved who are filthy and vulgar (Prov. 26:11; II Peter 2:22), who mock at God (Ps. 59:6), who are contemptible (II Sam. 9:8), and who will be outside the Holy City (Rev. 22:15). Jews used the term as a synonym for Gentiles (Matt. 15:26). The metaphor in this verse, however, referred to Jewish teachers who tried to impose legalism upon Gentile believers. The criticism of the false prophets within Israel aptly describes this group:

> His watchmen are blind: they are all ignorant, they are all dumb dogs, they cannot bark; sleeping, lying down, loving to slumber.
> Yea, they are greedy dogs which can never have enough, and they are shepherds that cannot understand: they all look to their own way, every one for his gain, from his quarter (Isa. 56:10–11).

2. Beware of evil workers

This warning describes their *conduct*. They were "workers" in that they aggressively promoted their beliefs. They were working for their own salvation, and they attempted to influence others to accept legalism as an additional requirement with faith as the grounds for divine acceptance. They were like the hypocritical Pharisees who travelled anywhere just to make one proselyte (Matt. 23:15).

They were also, however, "evil [*kakous*] workers." Elsewhere, Paul identified the Judaizers as "false apostles, deceitful workers, transforming themselves into the apostles of Christ" (II Cor. 11:13). Their work was marked by a heretical message and human motivations. Christ taught that good work done in His name by people who were not saved was really a work of iniquity (Matt. 7:21–23). They are ministers of righteousness based upon human pride and effort, not proclaimers of the divine righteousness which is imputed by grace through faith alone (II Cor. 11:15).

THE DANGER OF LEGALISM

3. Beware of the concision.

This warning denotes their *creed.* The term "concision" *(katatomēn)* refers to severe mutilation, a thorough cutting. This descriptive title must be seen in contrast to genuine circumcision *(peritomē)* which is based upon the same verb stem. The Judaizers were literally cutting down *(kata),* whereas circumcision involved a cutting around *(peri).* Physical mutilations, practiced in pagan idolatry, were prohibited by God through Moses (Lev. 21:5; I Kings 18:28).

In their zeal to physically circumcise their converts, the Judaizers were spiritually castrating them. They harmed people by their false teaching. They invited people to Christ while holding a Bible in one hand and a knife in the other. They proclaimed salvation by faith and works, which ultimately is a "works only" human religion. Paul pronounced this indictment upon them:

> As many as desire to make a fair show in the flesh, they constrain you to be circumcised; only lest they should suffer persecution for the cross of Christ.
> For neither they themselves who are circumcised keep the law; but desire to have you circumcised, that they may glory in your flesh (Gal. 6:12–13).

They are unsaved, under the curse of God (Gal. 1:6–9). They pervert the gospel by removing its gracious character.

C. Reason for Warning (3:3)

The connective "for" *(gar)* gives the reason for the three warnings. In this verse there is a contrast between the true circumcision and the false circumcision.

1. Definition of true circumcision

The personal pronoun "we" *(hēmeis)* has special stress. We believers in Christ, including circumcised Jews, circumcised Gentile proselytes, and uncircumcised Gentile converts, are the true spiritual children of Abraham (Gal. 3:26–29). The pronoun, of course, included both Paul and the church.

The verb "are" *(esmen)* manifests a dogmatic conviction that Paul was absolutely sure of the spiritual standing of his converts and himself. It was a present possession, enjoyed by all of them.

The phrase, "the circumcision" *(hē peritomē)*, is a synonym for the body of Christ, the true church, the family of God for this present age. It manifests the work of the Spirit of God within the heart of each believer at the time of regeneration. Paul elsewhere explained: "In Christ also ye are circumcised with the circumcision made without hands, in putting off the body of the sins of the flesh by the circumcision of Christ" (Col. 2:11). In the flesh, the presence or absence of circumcision distinguished between the Jew and the Gentile (Eph. 2:11), but spiritual circumcision involves the heart and the spirit (Rom. 2:28–29). Even God once said to the ritualistic Jews: "Circumcise yourselves to the Lord, and take away the foreskins of your heart" (Jer. 4:4). True circumcision removes the sin of the heart, not the skin of the flesh.

2. *Explanation of true circumcision*

The next three verbs, introduced by the relative pronoun "which," actually expound the meaning of spiritual circumcision.[6] Three aspects are given. *First,* genuine believers "worship God in the spirit." Constant worship is part of their daily behavior.[7] Christ declared that God is spirit and that men must worship Him in spirit and truth (John 4:24). The noun "spirit" could refer to either the Holy Spirit[8] or to the human spirit.[9] Regardless, both concepts are true. A believer worships the Father in his human spirit by the Holy Spirit who indwells him.

---

[6]There are actually three participles which follow a single definite article; thus they are three descriptions of the same group.

[7]Indicated by the present participle *hoi latreuontes.*

[8]Muller, *Epistles,* p. 107.

[9]KJV and RSV.

Second, genuine believers "rejoice in Christ Jesus." All saved people glory continually *(kauchōmenoi)*[10] in the finished redemptive work which the God-man accomplished through His death and resurrection. Paul confessed: "But God forbid that I should glory, save in the cross of our Lord Jesus Christ, by whom the world is crucified unto me, and I unto the world" (Gal. 6:14). To glory in Christ also means to admit that He is Jehovah God. God Himself admonished:

> Let not the wise man glory in his wisdom, neither let the mighty man glory in his might, let not the rich man glory in his riches:
> But let him that glorieth glory in this, that he understandeth and knoweth me, that I am the Lord which exercise loving-kindness, judgment, and righteousness, in the earth: for in these things I delight, saith the Lord (Jer. 9:23–24, cf. I Cor. 1:29–31).

Third, genuine believers "have no confidence in the flesh." When a person has such confidence, he thinks that he is good enough in himself and that he has sufficient ability to do whatever it takes to gain entrance into heaven.[11] Self-abasement is absolutely necessary to gain divine exaltation. The publican who cried out for mercy from a distance was justified by God, but the Pharisee who bragged about his religious achievements remained condemned (Luke 18:9–14).

II. IN CONFIDENCE (3:4–6)

The mention of "confidence" (3:3; cf. 3:4) serves as a transition from the first contrast to the second. On what basis can confidence be established? In this section, Paul sets forth the

[10]Indicated by the present participle.

[11]Indicated by the perfect participle *pepoithotes.* The tense of this verbal participle indicates a time when a person consciously comes to the conviction that he can do nothing to merit the righteousness of God and that he remains in that conviction throughout his lifetime.

criteria for spiritual excellence which he once trusted in his unsaved life.

A. Comparison of Confidence (3:4–6)

Paul never altered his message, but he did change his methods in order to minister to different groups (I Cor. 9:19–23). He reluctantly involved himself in boasting in order to disprove false allegations against him (II Cor. 11:1–12:11). In order to portray graphically the folly of self-confidence, he now used himself as an example. Two claims are set forth.

First, he asserted that he could have confidence ("Though I might also have confidence in the flesh"). The pronoun "I" *(egō)* puts great emphasis on the self. The adverb "also" links him with the Judaizers who built their ministries upon self-confidence. The verb "have" indicates that he could have boasted over many aspects of his life, not just one event.[12] The prepositional phrase "in the flesh" makes it clear that this is a confidence based upon human standards, not upon divine or biblical evaluations.

Second, he charged that he could have more confidence than anyone else in the world ("I more"). He did not just match the Judaizers or any other self-righteous group—he surpassed them. If God could have asked all human beings to line up before Him, from the most religious to the least, Paul would have been at the head of the line. He thus claimed to be superior to any religious devotee. This boast did not originate from any pride on his part; rather, he used this evaluation of his past as an argument to show the fallacy of such egomania.

B. Demonstration of Confidence (3:5–6)

Before he became a Christian, Paul's life was a spiritual

---

[12] It is a present participle *(echōn)* implied in a periphrastic construction.

paradox. He was at the same time both the best man and the worst man who had ever lived. He hated Christ and His followers; thus he became "a blasphemer, and a persecutor, and injurious" (I Tim. 1:13). In this passage, however, he set forth seven points of his human merit. The first four resulted from his genetic inheritance, whereas the last three reflected his personal choices. All of them, nevertheless, manifested one common essence: pride. Here can be found pride of race, family, patriotism, orthodoxy, zeal, and self-righteousness.

1. Circumcision

Circumcision was a sign of faith in the fulfillment of the Abrahamic covenant (Gen. 17:1–8; cf. 17:9–14). When the rite was first instituted, Abraham was ninety-nine years old and Ishmael was thirteen (Gen. 17:24–25). From that point on, however, a Jewish male child had to be circumcised on the eighth day after his birth (Gen. 17:12; Lev. 12:3). Gentiles became proselytes when they submitted to this religious surgery in their adult years. In conformity to the law, Jesus was circumcised on the eighth day (Luke 2:21), and so was Paul.

2. Stock of Israel

Paul was out "of the stock of Israel." He could trace his genealogical ancestry to the patriarchs, including Jacob whose name was changed to Israel by God (Gen. 35:10). He was not a Gentile proselyte. The term "stock" *(genous)* denotes kind, race, or generation.

God often identified Himself as the God of Abraham, Isaac, and Jacob. When the names of the twelve sons became known as the titles for the twelve tribes, then the term "Israel" came to be seen as the covenant name of the elect race (Rom. 11:1). Elsewhere Paul contrasted himself with the Judaizers: "Are they Hebrews? so am I. Are they Israelites? so am I. Are they the seed of Abraham? so am I." (II Cor. 11:22).

3. Tribe of Benjamin

Benjamin was the last of the twelve sons to be born to Jacob. In fact, his beloved wife Rachel died as she gave birth to this son (Gen. 35:16–18). This tribe gave to Israel her first king, Saul. It is very plausible that Paul's parents named him after this royal member of the tribe.[13]

The city of Jerusalem was located within the tribal area assigned to Benjamin (Judg. 1:21). In battle, the men of this tribe had the place of honor in the front line (Judg. 5:14). When the kingdom divided after the death of Solomon, the tribe of Benjamin remained loyal to the Davidic family which had descended from Judah.

4. Hebrew of the Hebrews

He was a Hebrew son born to Hebrew parents. Neither Paul nor his parents ever submitted to the influences of Hellenistic culture. He learned the Hebrew language and orthodox customs at an early age in his hometown of Tarsus and later received his rabbinical education in Hebrew at Jerusalem under the respected Gamaliel (Acts 22:2–3). Although he grew up in a Gentile city and learned both Greek and Aramaic, he did not become Hellenized as so many Jews had done (Acts 6:1).

5. Pharisee

After his three missionary journeys, Paul still confessed: "I am a Pharisee, the son of a Pharisee" (Acts 23:6). He thus contrasted himself with the other dominant Jewish sect, the Sadducees, who denied the existence of angels, the reality of spirit, and the physical resurrection of the dead (Acts 23:8). Phariseeism was "the most straitest sect" within Judaism (Acts 26:5). He was not only a member of this legalistic, orthodox group, but he was also its most zealous member. He once admitted: "And I profited in the Jews' religion above many my equals in mine own nation, being more exceedingly zealous of the traditions of my fathers" (Gal. 1:14).

---

[13]Remember that Paul's name was Saul before his conversion.

6. *Zealous*

In his "zeal" for his religious convictions, he was "persecuting the church." The present tense of the verb "persecuting" *(diōkōn)* shows the continuous activity of his determination to destroy Christianity and the vivid memory of those past days in his present experience. He was with those who firmly believed that Jesus Christ was a blasphemer, that His body had been stolen from the tomb by the disciples (Matt. 28:13–15), and that the followers of Christ comprised a heretical sect which deserved to be destroyed. He honestly thought that the killing of believers was a noble and meritorious service for God (cf. John 16:2). He was responsible for the martyrdom of the first Christian, Stephen (Acts 8:1), for forcing the apostles out of Jerusalem (Acts 8:1), and for imprisoning believers both in Jerusalem and in Damascus (Acts 8:3; 9:21). Christians were terrified by him (Acts 9:26).

His zeal and sincerity could never by questioned. Unfortunately, a person can be sincerely wrong. His explanation of Israel's blindness is actually a commentary upon his own unbelief of those ignorant days:

> For I bear them record that they have a zeal of God, but not according to knowledge.
> For they being ignorant of God's righteousness, and going about to establish their own righteousness, have not submitted themselves unto the righteousness of God (Rom. 10:2–3).

After his arrest in Jerusalem, he identified his past behavior with the present experience of the Jewish elders when he said that he "taught according to the perfect manner of the law of the fathers, and was zealous toward God, as ye all are this day" (Acts 22:3).

7. *Blameless*

The "righteousness which is in the law" could only be achieved by meticulous conformity to all of the positive and negative commandments.[14] Legal righteousness can only be granted to those who deserve it.

He asserted that he had become "blameless" *(amemptos)*. This word was used of proper Christian behavior in the world (2:15). He loved God and tried to serve Him to the best of his ability. No one could accuse him of being slothful in his attempts to keep the law. He was not perfect—in fact, he sinned—but doubtless he immediately offered a proper sacrifice for his atonement.

Questions for Discussion

1. Are Christians given enough warnings about false teachers and erroneous doctrine? What are the best ways to alert them?

2. What is involved in declaring the whole counsel of God? How does this relate to the correct procedure of discipleship?

3. What contemporary groups correspond to the ancient Judaizers? What are the modern equivalents to the issue of circumcision?

4. How can God be worshiped in the spirit? What is the difference between proper order and legalistic formality?

5. In what ways do people put confidence in the flesh? How can their pride be exposed?

6. How do people recite their religious pedigrees today? Is this possible through pride of denomination?

7. How can people be sincerely wrong in their religious practice? How can such people be won to Christ?

---

[14]They were codified into 613 separate regulations.

10

The Joy of Salvation
Philippians 3:7–14

In the first part of this chapter (3:1–6), Paul contrasted himself with the legalistic Judaizers, but in this middle section he reveals his new relationship to Jesus Christ. Two aspects of his salvation are given here: justification (3:7–9) and sanctification (3:10–14).

I. IN JUSTIFICATION (3:7–9)

Justification is the act of God whereby He declares to be righteous that sinner who has received the righteousness of God by faith in Jesus Christ. Its essense is grace (Rom. 3:24), its source is God (Rom. 3:26), its means is faith (Rom. 3:28), its grounds is the blood of Christ (Rom. 5:9), its sphere is Christ Jesus (I Cor. 6:11), its agent is the Holy Spirit (I Cor. 6:11), and its evidence is works (James 2:24).

At the time of justification or conversion, a sinner must reject the proud efforts of self and accept the gracious provision of Christ. Paul did exactly that. The strong adversative "but" (*alla*) shows the continuity between the first two parts of this chapter and the contrast between Paul's past and present.

A. He Rejected Self

The phrase "what things" (*hatina*) refers to the seven points of Paul's past religious position and practice (3:5–6).

They had produced a legalistic sense of confidence within his life. The noun "gain" *(kerdē)* is in the plural and thus should be read as "gains" (cf. 1:21; *kerdos).* The apostle had looked upon each individual achievement as a separate gain. The verb "were" shows that these things were done in his unsaved early life as a Pharisee.

1. He esteemed his gains as loss (3:7)

His assets became liabilities; his credits suddenly were transferred into the debits column. The verb "I counted" indicates that he made a conscious decision to repudiate his religious and racial inheritance and successes, and that he continued to view his past in an unfavorable light.[1] This new outlook occurred at the time of his repentance. Just as Jesus Christ had to esteem His divine wealth as loss in order to secure the foundation of salvation (2:6), so every sinner must regard his spiritual riches as nothing in order to gain personal salvation.[2]

The apostle counted his gains to be "loss" *(zēmian).* Since the word is in the singular, he grouped all of his gains together into one and treated them as a unified loss. There was nothing meritorious in any one of them. Christ gave this difference between gain and loss:

> For whosoever will save his life shall lose it: and whosoever will lose his life for my sake shall find it.
>
> For what is a man profited, if he shall gain the whole world, and lose his own soul? or what shall a man give in exchange for his soul? (16:25–26).

The word translated "loss" *(zēmian)* was also used of the loss and damage suffered by the ship on which Paul was taken a prisoner to Rome (Acts 27:10, 21). The cargo was thrown overboard and the ship broke up (Acts 27:38, 41). In like

---

[1]The verb is a perfect middle indicative, *hēgēmai.*

[2]The verbs "thought" (2:6) and "counted" (3:7) come from the same stem, *hēgeomai.*

manner, a sinner must discard his pride in order to rescue his soul.

The prepositional phrase "for Christ" gives the reason for the radical rejection of self. Man must do it to receive the righteousness of the Savior.

2. *He suffered loss (3:8b)*

At his conversion, Paul not only counted his religious gains to be loss, but he also "suffered the loss of all things." The verb tense *(ezēmiōthēn)* looks back to a definite time in his past.[3] It cost the young Pharisee to become a Christian. He lost his status within Judaism, his reputation, and his opportunity for wealth and fame. He experienced ostracism, bodily harm, death threats, and property destruction (cf. Heb. 10:34). He may have forfeited his Jewish birthright and family inheritance.

The inclusive phrase "all things" goes beyond the areas listed as gains (3:5–6). It embraces all spheres of human experience. His conversion produced radical changes in all of his personal and social relationships.

Why did he do it? Again he explained ("for whom"). He did it because Christ had done something for him. To have everything without Christ is to have nothing, but to have Christ is to possess everything. The reason behind his conversion was not intellectual or psychological: rather, it was christological. It was for the sake of Christ.

3. *He esteems his gains as dung (3:8b)*

In these two verses, Paul revealed his present attitude toward his past by using the same verb *(hēgeomai)* three times; however, he made a sharp contrast by twice changing the tense from "counted" *(hēgēmai)* to "count" *(hēgoumai)*.[4] After twenty-five years of Christian experience, he still deprecated his self-righteous effort in the same way that he did

---

[3]Aorist passive indicative.
[4]From the perfect tense to the present.

when he was born again. In genuine conversion, a believer repudiates legalism for both the imputation and the maintenance of his salvation.

The graphic term "dung" *(skubala)* has two possible derivations. *First,* it could come from the noun stem for body excrement *(skor). Second,* it may refer to the food leftovers which were thrown to the dogs (from *ek kunas ballō).* In either case, it points to that which must be discarded as useless waste.

4. He rejected his righteousness (3:9a)

Paul had boasted about his achievements in order to become righteous in the sight of God and man. He once saw himself as "blameless" concerning the "righteousness which is in the law" (3:6). He knew that he had righteousness, but he now recognized that he had the wrong kind. He needed to dispose of the kind of righteousness which he possessed ("not having mine own righteousness, which is of the law"). He used the emphatic possessive adjective "mine own" *(emēn)* to contrast his righteousness with that of God.

He finally perceived that no one is righteous in himself before God; thus no one can produce righteous acts which can bring divine salvation to him (Rom. 3:10). He now understood the prophetic declaration: "But we are all as an unclean thing, and all our righteousnesses are as filthy rags" (Isa. 64:6). Solomon observed: "There is a generation that are pure in their own eyes, and yet is not washed from their filthiness" (Prov. 30:12). The most subtle form of moral impurity is a self-righteous life style, and the person who has this blinded opinion of self is the most difficult one to reach with the gospel message.

B. He Accepted Christ

The exclamation "Yea, doubtless" shows the intensity of his new conviction. Actually, it is composed of five Greek particles *(alla, men, oun, ge, kai)* which respectively have the translation "but, indeed, therefore, at least, even." They set up a striking contrast between the old and the new outlooks on righteousness.

His acceptance of salvation through Christ is now seen in four aspects.

1. He now knew Christ (3:8a)

He repudiated his past legalistic efforts "for the excellency of the knowledge of Christ Jesus my Lord." Salvation is not based upon ignorance; rather, it involves knowledge. A sinner must know something to be saved, and he also must know someone. He must know intellectually that Jesus Christ is both God and man, that He died for the guilt and penalty of his sin, that He rose physically from the dead, that He is the only Savior of mankind, and that he cannot do anything to save himself. He must then know Christ experientially by believing in Him, by entrusting himself completely to the saving care of the Lord.

Christ criticized the religious leaders for not knowing Him nor the Father (John 7:28; 8:55). In His prayer to the Father, He defined salvation: "And this is life eternal, that they might know thee the only true God, and Jesus Christ, whom thou hast sent" (John 17:3). This knowledge comes by personal commitment and inner relationship. For example, Mary knew that she was legally betrothed to Joseph, but yet she did not "know" a man intimately in sexual relationships (Luke 1:34). Saving knowledge thus stems from a choice to give oneself completely over to another.

God knew Israel by choosing it from among the nations of the earth (Amos 3:2). God "knows them that are his" today because He chose them in eternity past and now indwells them (II Tim. 2:19; cf. Eph. 1:4). Paul delineated the salvation experience of the Galatians in these terms: "But now, after that ye have known God, or rather are known of God" (Gal. 4:9). Saving knowledge thus is reciprocal. When it occurs, a man then knows God as his father and Christ as his Savior, and God now knows the believing sinner as His child.

Paul's salvation experience began when he asked this searching question on the Damascus road: "Who art thou, Lord?" (Acts 9:5). When he knew the answer, he was then born again. Such knowledge has more "excellency" than all of the self-righteous acts of all men put together.

2. He won Christ (3:8b)

The apostle lost in order that he might gain. He lost self and gained Christ. He lost sin and gained righteousness. He lost that which was human and gained that which was divine. He lost temporal things and gained eternal things.

The conjunction "that" *(hina)* gives the purpose for the rejection of his selfish gains. The verb "I may win" is actually based upon the same stem as the noun "gain" *(kerdē)*; thus, Paul wanted to gain Christ *(kerdēsō)*. He not only gained Christ in that one crucial event, but also for an entire lifetime.[5] The active voice of the verb shows the human responsibility in the appropriation of salvation.

In salvation, men gain "Christ." They gain Him, not just things from Him. The eternal destiny of the believer is to be with Christ, not just to be in heaven (I Thess. 4:17).

3. He was found in Christ (3:9a)

Paul also wanted to "be found in Christ" *(eurethō en autōi)*. The passive voice of this verb shows that a believing sinner has been put into Christ by God. The human gaining and the divine placing occur at the same moment. The sphere of acceptance comes from one's position in Christ. When a person is in Him, he has been blessed with all spiritual blessings (Eph. 1:3). In Christ, he has divine election, predestination, acceptance, redemption, forgiveness, inheritance, and sealing (Eph. 1:4–14). He can rejoice in his new position: "Therefore if any man be in Christ, he is a new creature; old things are passed away; behold all things are become new" (II Cor. 5:17).

---

[5]It can be viewed as either an ingressive or a constative aorist.

THE JOY OF SALVATION

4. He possessed the righteousness of God (3:9b)

In Christ, Paul had divine righteousness ("but [having] that which..."). Four aspects of this possession are set forth. *First,* its means is "through the faith of Christ" *(dia pisteōs Christou).* The person and redemptive work of Christ was the means of the saving faith (cf. Rom. 3:22, 28–31).[6]

Second, its source is out "of God" *(ek theou).* In salvation, a person becomes a partaker of the divine nature; thus God imputes to him positional righteousness (II Peter 1:4). The believing sinner is just as righteous as Christ because he has been "made the righteousness of God in him" (II Cor. 5:21).

Third, its basis is "faith" *(epi tēi pistei).* The righteous position rests "upon" *(epi)* the foundation of faith or trust, not upon pride or self-effort.

Fourth, its sphere is "in him," namely, Christ. Before God, a person is either found in Adam (self) or in Christ (Rom. 5:12–21). The former brings condemnation, whereas the latter guarantees justification.

II. IN SANCTIFICATION (3:10–14)

Christ said: "I am come that they might have life, and that they might have it more abundantly" (John 10:10). When a believing sinner has justification he obtains life (cf. 3:7–9), but when he works at sanctification he gains the abundant life (cf. 3:10–14). Getting saved is like getting married; it is just the beginning of a growing, knowing, sharing relationship.

A. The Goals of Sanctification (3:10)

The words of purpose, "that I may know," are the translation of an articular infinitive *(tou gnōnai).*[7] This purpose can-

---

[6]The noun "Christ" is regarded as an objective genitive.

[7]The genitive article *tou* with an infinitive shows purpose. It is a constative aorist infinitive in that it views all of life's experiences grouped together.

not be fulfilled unless the truth of the prior verses is a living reality (3:7–9). Paul thus counted all selfish gain to be loss so that he might win Christ and be found in Him in order that he might know Him. Justification must precede sanctification.

The verb indicates personal, experiential knowledge. Three objects of that knowledge are now set forth.

1. To know Him

There is a difference between objective and personal knowledge of a person. The former deals with facts about a man, whereas the latter stresses intimate acquaintance. For example, all Americans know who the President is, but very few know him personally.

Paul knew that he had salvation; now he wanted to know the Savior. This goal is a lifelong pursuit because the divine person of the Son of God is inexhaustible. Men are not known as objects are known. Persons are known as they reveal themselves to others. Christ said that He would manifest Himself to those believers who loved Him and who had kept His commandments (John 14:21).

Believers can grow in grace and in the knowledge of Christ through a diligent study of the Scriptures which testify of Christ (John 5:39; II Peter 3:18). As they see Him and begin to know Him through the written Word, that truth will transform their personalities into conformity to Christ (II Cor. 3:18).

2. To know the power of His resurrection

The same "power" (dunamin) which raised Jesus Christ out of physical death also raised the believing sinner out of spiritual death, and this power presently operates within the believer to give him daily victory over sin (Eph. 1:18–2:7). Paul prayed that believers might perceive this truth (Eph. 1:15–20).

By spiritual identification with Christ through the baptism in the Holy Spirit, all believing sinners are crucified, buried, and raised together with Christ (Rom. 6:3–10). Just as sin and death no longer have dominion over the living, resurrected Savior, so the believer should by faith claim that divine victory for himself. The apostle charged: "Likewise reckon ye also yourselves to be dead indeed unto sin, but alive unto God through Jesus Christ our Lord" (Rom. 6:11).

3. To know the fellowship of His sufferings

Jesus announced to His disciples: "Ye shall drink indeed of my cup, and be baptized with the baptism that I am baptized with" (Matt. 20:23). That cup involved agony and suffering, and that baptism embraced death in the will of God (Matt. 26:36–46). All of the apostles suffered physically and subsequently died as martyrs.

Paul likewise wanted to know "the fellowship of his sufferings." No believer can die for sins as Christ did, but he can suffer for the sake of righteousness as he permits Christ to live out His life through him. Peter encouraged his readers: "For even hereunto were ye called: because Christ also suffered for us, leaving us an example, that ye should follow his steps" (I Peter 2:21). All believers who deny themselves, take up their crosses daily, and follow Christ will share in His sufferings (Matt. 16:24). This unique fellowship will involve suffering for doing well (I Peter 2:20), for righteousness (I Peter 3:14), for the name of Christ (I Peter 4:14), as a Christian (I Peter 4:16), and according to the will of God, (I Peter 4:19).

Such total resignation to the will of God means "being made conformable unto his death." It is saying to God: "Not my will, but thine be done." Just as Christ was in the "form" (morphē) of God, so the believer should be "conformed" (summorphoumenos) to His death. The essence of the cross-death should be the goal of each Christian (cf. 2:8). The present tense of the participle indicates that this joint conformity should be a progressive daily drive in each life; thus Paul could say: "I die daily" (I Cor. 15:31). The passive voice of the participle shows that the Holy Spirit causes this transformation to occur.

The order of the verse (living Savior, resurrection, death) reflects the experience of the believer, whereas it was just the opposite in the historical occurrence. Christ suffered before He was raised, but a believer will suffer if he manifests resurrection power in his daily living.

B. The Expectation in the Goals (3:11)

This verse has two possible interpretations. Both are consistent within the context of the teaching of this epistle.

1. To be sensitive in the present[8]

The emphasis here is on a spiritual resurrection (cf. Rom. 6:7–10). Paul wrote: "Awake thou that sleepest, and *arise from the dead (anasta ek tōn nekrōn)*, and Christ shall give thee light" (Eph. 5:14). The italicized words correspond to the phrase under discussion, "the resurrection of the dead" *(tēn exanastasin tōn nekrōn)*. Since Paul wrote Ephesians and Philippians at the same time, these two verses could easily be a commentary upon each other.

The conditional character ("if by any means") only indicates the uncertainty of Paul's immediate future. He knew that he would have to keep fighting against his sin nature (3:12; cf. I Cor. 9:27). Muller sees the phrase as an expression of his "humble expectation and modest self-confidence."[9]

2. To be accepted in the future

The emphasis here is on a physical resurrection (I Cor. 15:51–58; I Thess. 4:13–18). It is literally "the out resurrection" *(exanastasin)*. When Christ returns, living believers will be translated and dead Christians will be raised. The unsaved will be resurrected later; thus this would be a resurrection out from among the unsaved who would remain dead (Rev. 20:5).

[8]Author's view.
[9]Jac. J. Muller, *The Epistles of Paul to the Philippians and to Philemon*, p. 118.

Paul did not doubt the reality of Christ's return, the translation of living saints, or the resurrection of the dead. The conditional character of the verse thus points to the uncertainty as to whether he would be alive or dead in that day. Since the return of Christ was imminent, Paul wanted to be spiritually ready at all times. He wanted to be praised before the Savior, not ashamed (Matt. 24:44–47; I John 2:28).

C. The Attitudes Behind the Expectation (3:12)

Paul was neither complacent nor apathetic in his spirituality. In honest introspection, he revealed three basic attitudes that controlled his holy ambition.

1. He had not received everything

He admitted that he had not yet "attained." Literally, it reads "received" (*elabon*). He had not yet received everything that God had in store for him. In the thirty years since his conversion, Paul had enjoyed many times of blessing, but there were still more experiences ahead in which he came to know the Lord in a new way. God is a giving God, and He will continue to give to those who want more.

2. He had not become everything

He admitted that he was not yet "perfect." This is actually a verbal construction: "Not that . . . I have already been perfected" (*teteleiōmai*).[10] The verb conveys the idea of a decisive past event with the results of that experience continuing into the present. He knew that he was not in a perfected state, with no room for personal, spiritual development.

If Paul, the greatest of the apostles, who had already served the Lord for thirty years, had not yet achieved perfection, then no Christian can ever reach this plateau in this life. This verse repudiates any denominational distinctive which teaches sinless perfectionism or a permanent state of practical holiness.

[10]Perfect passive indicative.

3. He had not done everything

He had present ambition to improve ("I follow after"). This verb indicates hard pursuit, such as a hunter following the tracks of his prey. The fact that he had not yet "attained" and was not yet "perfect" did not discourage him; rather, they encouraged him to work harder at his goals.

He wanted to "apprehend that for which also [he] was apprehended of Christ Jesus." The verb "apprehend" means to lay hold of and to pull down *(katelēphthēn)*. It is comparable to making a tackle on the football field from behind. Christ pursued Paul until He caught him on the road to Damascus (Acts 9); now Paul was pursuing his Savior. Christ had a divine purpose for saving Paul and for calling him into apostolic service. Paul knew that fact, and he wanted to do everything that God had planned for him to accomplish. He wanted to be like a marathon runner who hit the tape with complete exhaustion and who could humbly exclaim: "I have finished my course" (II Tim. 4:7).

D. The Ambition in the Attitudes (3:13–14)

The abrupt insertion of the vocative ("Brethren") is used to draw attention to his conclusion. The Judaizers did not have the joy of either justification or sanctification. Paul definitely had the former, and he wanted the latter. The joy of sanctification is based upon daily ambition and achievement. It is described here in four concepts.

1. To be honest about oneself

He knew that he had not yet achieved the total divine purpose for his life ("I count not myself to have apprehended"). The verb "apprehend" *(logizomai)* means to think something through to a conclusion.[11] The pronouns "I" *(egō)* and "my-

---

[11]Although translated, "I count," it is a different verb than the one given earlier *(hēgoumai; 3:8).*

self" *(emauton)* are very emphatic. They stress that Paul had evaluated his own spiritual condition, not that he had accepted the opinions of others.

2. To forget the past

Paul daily was "forgetting those things which are behind." No person can erase from his memory what has transpired before, but he can keep the past from controlling the present and the future. When God forgives our sins He still remembers what they were, but He does not hold them against us. A believer thus must not permit the past to cause him depression or overconfidence in the present.

The "things which are behind" include Paul's past Pharisaical life which he had just recounted. In progressive sanctification, a believer must not look upon his unsaved past with so much shame or pride that he fails to see Christ. In the same sense, he must not view his Christian past with either disdain or satisfaction. He must not look on his own things (2:4).

3. To reach for the future

Someone has said: "Today is the first day of the rest of your life." For believers, the best is yet to come. They should face the future with anticipation and joy.

Paul was "reaching forth unto those things which are before." The verb "reaching" *(epekteinomenos)* denotes an athlete who runs without swerving off course and who strains his entire body to cross the finish line (Acts 20:24; I Cor. 9:26). It was a spiritual exercise which occurred every day in the apostle's life.[12]

The "things which are before" have already been discussed. They include a personal knowledge of Christ, victory over sin and self, and more personal growth and achievement.

For Paul, at least three other epistles remained to be writ-

---

[12]Note the present tense of the participles.

ten (I and II Timothy, Titus). A work on Crete needed to be established (Titus 1:5). A life needed to be given in martyrdom.

4. To press toward the mark

With all of his holy ambition, the apostle wanted to do "one thing" (3:13). He earnestly desired to "press toward the mark for the prize of the high calling of God in Christ Jesus." The verb "press" *(diōkō)* describes vigorous, concentrated pursuit.

Paul was a man with a goal ("toward the mark"). He knew who he was and where he was going. One author wrote: "Let us lay aside every weight, and the sin which doth so easily beset us, and let us run with patience the race that is set before us, looking unto Jesus the author and finisher of our faith" (Heb. 12:1–2). All believers must realize that both God and others are watching them; at the same time they must fix their eyes on Christ. Their goal is to be like Him.

A "prize" *(brabeion)* will be given for success. At the Greek games, the winner of a race was summoned from the stadium floor to the seat of the judge. A wreath of leaves was placed upon his head. At Athens, the winner was also given five hundred coins, free meals, and a front row seat at the theater. These prizes were temporary, but believers can obtain an eternal and incorruptible prize (I Cor. 9:26).

This human endeavor has been made possible by "the high calling of God in Christ Jesus." God has chosen men in Christ Jesus to be saved and to be sanctified. The prize itself is a gracious gift, but attainment of the goal requires human effort. The adverb "high" *(anō)* means "upward." God's goals for the believer are always forward and upward. They are designed to strengthen and to improve him.

Questions for Discussion

1. Do people suffer the loss of anything today when they profess salvation?

2. What is the difference between spiritual position and spiritual practice? Which is more important?

3. What is involved in genuine saving faith? Is repentance essential? How would you define imputation of righteousness?

4. How can believers know Christ personally? How much time is involved? How can church programs help or hinder?

5. Are all Christians victorious over sin today? Why not? What can be done to attain this goal?

6. Why are believers sometimes depressed? Apathetic? Why do they often lack ambition?

7. How can you press toward the mark for your life? Name some of your failures. How can these be overcome?

11

The Joy of Maturity
Philippians 3:15–21

All Christians must confess: "Please be patient with me; God is not through with me yet." Spiritual birth presupposes growth into maturity. Such advancement implies deficiencies which need correction, weaknesses which need strengthening, and ignorance which needs education. The local church which prospers has members with mutual forbearance and understanding toward each other.

In this section, the apostle challenged the believers to experience the joy of maturity.

I. THE GOALS FOR THE CHURCH (3:15–16)

The conjunction "therefore" (*oun*) joins this section to the previous one. Paul wanted his personal aims to become the goals for the Philippians. Two are given.

A. Same Mind (3:15)

1. The command

Three features of this command are set forth. *First*, it included both Paul and his readers. The exhortation ("let us . . . be thus minded") shows that the apostle identified himself with the church and that he needed to be stimulated to further growth as they did.[1] It literally reads: "Let us keep on thinking" *(phronōmen)*. It is the same verb as that used for thinking the same thing ("likeminded"), the one thing ("one mind"), and the mind of Christ ("the mind . . . which was also in Christ") (2:5).

Second, it could only be obeyed by those who were mature and who were maturing ("as many as be perfect"). The qualitative adjective "as many as" *(hosoi)* shows that only a select group of believers would respond to the apostolic appeal. All Christians, unfortunately, remain in a state of spiritual infancy throughout their lives. The adjectival title "perfect" *(teleioi)* does not contradict Paul's earlier denial of personal perfection (3:12). A mature believer knows where he is in the divine order of spiritual progress and perceives that he can still develop further. For example, a perfect eight-year-old child is at the right stage of physical, emotional, and intellectual maturity for his age bracket, but he is still maturing toward a nine-year-old goal. Perfect believers are open to instruction and admonition (I Cor. 2:6; 14:20). They have moral discernment and are able to receive the "strong meat" of the Scriptures (Heb. 5:14). The believer has positional perfection in Christ, but he must strive to attain ethical perfection (Heb. 10:14).

Third, the command to be "thus minded" was directed toward one purpose. The word "thus" is normally translated as "this" *(touto)*. This demonstrative pronoun points back to the apostle's specified goal of pressing toward the mark, of doing all that God planned for you to do, and of becoming all that God had designed for His children.

2. *The correction*

Some Christians blindly think that they do not need to improve or that they can mature through legalism ("and if in anything ye be otherwise minded"). They take a position other *(heterōs)* than that lived or prescribed by Paul.

---

[1] It is a hortatory subjunctive (present tense).

Someone has said that a person convinced against his own will is of the same opinion still. After all that Paul had taught in this epistle and after describing his own spiritual condition which still needed improvement, what more could the apostle say to change their wills? Did they actually think that they were better than he was? In this situation, he simply turned them over to divine conviction ("God shall reveal even this unto you"). The means of illumination would be the teaching of the Holy Spirit, the observation of the growth of mature believers in grace, and the rod of chastisement.

B. Same Walk (3:16)

Paul admitted that both the church and he had made significant progress in their spiritual life. The concept "whereto" (eis ho) literally means "into which." They had moved into a doctrinal position and a behavioral pattern which were being threatened by the legalists. The verb "we have already attained" shows that they had arrived at this plateau after much effort and experience.[2] The Judaizers, however, charged that they had to advance beyond simple faith by means of a complex legalistic system. Elsewhere, Paul castigated the fallacy of this maneuver: "Are ye so foolish? having begun in the Spirit, are ye now made perfect by the flesh?" (Gal. 3:3).

God has only one way of salvation, and He likewise has only one means of sanctification. Both Jews and Gentiles alike are saved by faith in Christ alone and they become holy by total submission to the Holy Spirit who produces His fruit through them. The standard of the Christian walk is here described as "the same rule." The noun "rule" (kanoni) transliterates as "canon." Just as the Bible alone is the basis of evangelical faith and practice, so these standards should provide the guidelines for daily living.

The verbs "walk" and "mind" argue for constant obedience to the directives of Paul rather than to those of the le-

---

[2]Aorist active indicative: ephthasamen.

galists. The exhortations emphasize duration, especially since they are really present infinitives *(stoichein* and *phronein). First,* he wanted them to "walk" according to the same principles which he had just discussed. The same verb is used in this admonition: "If we live in the Spirit, let us also walk in the Spirit" (Gal. 5:25). A Spirit-controlled walk is void of dissension and petty jealousy; rather, it is marked by love and concern for others (Gal. 5:22–6:5).

Second, he desired them to "mind the same thing" *(to auto phronein).* This is the exact phrase found in the apostle's initial plea for unity: "Fulfil ye my joy, that ye be likeminded" (2:2). There can be no joy if there is static immaturity and selfish competition within the bounds of legalism.

II. THE APOSTASY OF THE JUDAIZERS (3:17–19)

Paul ended this chapter with a warning, just as he began it (3:1–2). The direct address ("Brethren") also served to alert them and to form a transition to this new subject.

Apostasy is a departure from a moral and doctrinal standard. In this section, Paul established himself as the spiritual yardstick by which the heretical legalists were to be measured.

A. The Standard of Orthodoxy (3:17)

1. Paul

With all humility, the apostle could confidently admonish them: "Be followers together of me." He wanted them to become and thus to be as he was. He knew what God had done in his life, that his theology and practice were sound, and that they needed an objective, visible, human goal. With all of his apostolic authority he could make this pronouncement because he knew that he was following Christ (I Cor. 11:1).

The verb "be" *(ginesthe)* indicates that they were to keep becoming what he was. The noun "followers together" *(summimētai)* literally means "joint imitators." The term "mimic" is based upon it.

STAND UNITED IN JOY

2. Others

The first imperative was focused on Paul, but the second command was directed toward others. The charge "mark" *(skopeite)* calls for careful scrutiny. The English word *scope* (e.g., microscope) comes from this Greek term. Its present tense suggests that the Philippians were to set their sights constantly on those who were in their midst, especially since Paul was absent from them.

There is some disagreement as to whether this group which they were told to observe was a good or a bad example ("them which walk so"). *First,* it could refer to men like Timothy and Epaphroditus who would soon be in the midst of the church. There were also Pauline followers among the bishops and deacons (1:1). John advised his readers to mimic the good Demetrius rather than the bad Diotrephes (III John 9–12).

Second, a less plausible possibility is that the group could have been the poor example of the Judaizers (3:18–19). Since the epistle was addressed to the entire membership, the church had to be vigilant in its evaluation of speakers who came from the outside. Paul did use the same verb ("mark") to warn another church about false teachers:

> Now I beseech you, brethren, mark them which cause divisions and offences contrary to the doctrine which ye have learned; and avoid them.
>
> For they that are such serve not our Lord Jesus Christ, but their own belly; and by good words and fair speeches deceive the hearts of the simple (Rom. 16:17–18).

In either case, Paul offered his associates and himself as an "example" by which others should be tested. There is a noticeable switch from "me" to "us." The corporate group of the apostolic team thus served as a single standard, manifesting the unity of the apostle with his friends. The word "example" *(tupon)* is normally transliterated as a "type." It was the impression or the stamp made by an industrial die. It was used of the nail prints in the hands of Christ, left by the hard blows (John 20:25). Paul and his associates thus became a mold into which the lives of others could be poured and conformed.

B. The Violation of Orthodoxy (3:18–19)

The explanatory conjunction "for" *(gar)* gives the reason for the two commands just given (3:17). Imitation and vigilance were needed because "many" false teachers were walking in the midst of the churches. Believers must examine the spirits and perceive the difference between the spirit of truth and the spirit of error (I John 4:1–6). They should not be gullible and accept all preachers as genuine.

Whenever Paul was in their church, he kept telling them about the imminent invasion of heretics ("of whom I have told you often"). In this epistle, he was forced to warn them once again ("and now tell you"). His love for Christ, the truth, and the Philippian believers can be seen in his compassionate concern ("even weeping"). Tears came down from his eyes as he dictated his letter. He did not want them to fall prey to the spiritual lions who were prowling about in order to devour unsuspecting Christians (cf. I Peter 5:8–9). No father wants to see his children go astray. In such an attitude, Paul warned the Ephesian church about the inroads of apostasy for three years "night and day with tears" (Acts 20:31).

This unscrupulous group of false teachers is described in five ways.

1. Enemies of the cross of Christ

The "enemies of the cross" manifested their hostility to the redemptive message of Christ's death and resurrection by insisting that faith alone in Christ is not sufficient to save. They expressed faith in the person of Christ, but not in his finished work. They contended that circumcision and obedience to the Mosaic law needed to be added to faith in order to receive justification (Acts 15:1). If righteousness, or any part of it, is dependent upon legalism, then the value of Christ's death is negated (Gal. 2:21; 5:2, 4). The concept of salvation by works is contrary to the principle of divine grace (II Cor. 11:13–15; Gal. 5:10).

2. Their end is destruction

These legalists are lost and destined for perdition. The "end" *(telos)* refers to the conclusion of the acceptance of their message. If a person who has embraced legalism dies, then he will go to Hades to await the final resurrection, the Great White Throne judgment, and eternal consignment to the lake of fire.

The term "destruction" *(apōleia)* is based upon the same stem which is used to form words like *perish* and *lost* (Luke 19:10; I Cor. 1:18). The unsaved treat the message of the cross with intellectual contempt because they already are perishing (I Cor. 1:18). If they do not exercise repentant faith in Christ, then their living convictions will be confirmed at their death. In hell they will not experience extinction, but the total loss of well-being. Peter described them in this fashion:

> ... there shall be false teachers among you, who privily shall bring in damnable *(apōleias)* heresies, even denying the Lord that bought them and bring upon themselves swift destruction *(apōleian)*.
> And many shall follow their pernicious *(apōleiais)* ways: by reason of whom the way of truth shall be evil spoken of.
> And through covetousness shall they with feigned words make merchandise of you: whose judgment now of a long time lingereth not, and their damnation *(apōleia)* slumbereth not (II Peter 2:1–3).

These are destructive men destined for destruction.[3]

---

[3]Notice the various usages of *apolēia* in the Petrine passage.

3. Their god is their belly

These false preachers were in the ministry for what they could get out of it. Peter warned about elders who would take a pastorate for "filthy lucre" (I Peter 5:2). Paul likewise cautioned his readers about greedy ministers (I Tim. 6:3–10). Their belly became their god in that they served their worldly appetites (Rom. 16:18).

One reason why Paul surrendered his right to be supported financially by his converts was to avoid the suspicion that he was only interested in their money (I Cor. 9:1–18). In order to show that salvation was a divine gift, he offered his apostolic services at no charge. Unfortunately, his critics turned this gracious gesture into an argument against his apostleship (II Cor. 11:7–9; 12:13). They claimed that God financially prospered all successful preachers (I Tim. 6:5). This assertion is ridiculous in that Christ Himself experienced no material rewards in this life.

4. They glory in their shame

They gloried in those things of which they should have been ashamed. They boasted in the flesh, in the physical rite of circumcision, and in the legalistic efforts of self. They bragged about the number of people they were able to get to submit to circumcision. Of them Paul wrote: " ... [they] desire to have you circumcised, that they may glory in your flesh" (Gal. 6:13).

5. They mind earthly things

Believers frequently are castigated for being so heavenly-minded that they are no earthly good. Although Christians are supposed to seek those spiritual things which are above (Col. 3:1), they are not to ignore their human obligations.

The converse, however, is more usually true. Men are often so earthly-minded that they never think about heavenly matters. The Judaizers attempted to spoil the church "through philosophy and vain deceit, after the tradition of men, after the rudiments of the world, and not after Christ"

(Col. 2:8). The legalists attempted to force Gentile believers into a legalistic calendar where they would "observe days, and months, and times, and years," which manifested the elements or standards of a lost world (Gal. 4:3, 9–10). They tried to impose a restricted diet upon the church in which certain foods could not be touched, tasted, or handled (Col. 2:21–22). This legalistic conformity replaced grace and faith as the basis for justification and sanctification. A man who trusts himself must always look down at the earth rather than up into heaven.

III. THE GLORIFICATION OF BELIEVERS (3:20–21)

Legalism may tell a person how to live, but it cannot prepare him for death. Since it is based upon self effort, it is powerless to raise a man out of death. It is at this very point that the insufficiency of legalism is laid bare.

In contrast, the believing sinner has put his trust in the Christ who conquered death and Hades through His resurrection. In this life, he can look forward to death and resurrection because it will be the climax of his maturing process.

In these closing verses on the joy of total salvation, Paul described three features about the third of the three stages in the believer's spiritual experience (justification, sanctification, and glorification).

A. Our Citizenship Is in Heaven (3:20a)

1. Its meaning

The old English term "conversation" (*politeuma*) has the literal meaning of "citizenship."[4] The residents of Philippi were actually citizens of Rome. They constituted a Roman colony within the region of Macedonia. Away from Rome they were still Romans (Acts 16:12, 21); thus they fully understood the significance of this spiritual metaphor.

---

[4]It is based upon the Greek word for "city" (*polis*), often found within the names of American cities.

Christians likewise constitute a colony of heaven on earth. They have double citizenship. Paul was in the kingdom of God, and yet he claimed and used the rights of his Roman citizenship (Acts 16:37; 22:25–29).

The possessive pronoun "our" is very emphatic and stresses the joint possession of heavenly citizenship by Paul and the church in contrast to the earthly plight of the Judaizers.[5]

2. *Its location*

It literally is "in the heavens" *(en ouranois).*[6] In a general sense they are heavenly citizens, but specifically, their residency is the Holy City (Rev. 21:2, 10). The Philippians likewise were members of the empire, but they belonged to the city of Rome. Men of faith, like Abraham, looked for this city "whose builder and maker is God" (Heb. 11:10). Christ has prepared rooms for believers within this city which God has constructed for His own (John 14:2–3; Heb. 11:16).

Peter charged that Christians have an "inheritance incorruptible and undefiled, and that fadeth not away, reserved in heaven" (I Peter 1:4). Christ admonished the members of the kingdom of heaven to lay up treasure in heaven (Matt. 6:20).

The verb "is" indicates that this citizenship was a present possession. It is the same verb used to describe Christ's "being" in the form of God (2:6; *huparchei).* Just as the deity of Christ can never be diminished, so the heavenly citizenship of the believer can never be taken away. It exists now and forever.

B. Our Savior Can Come Soon (3:20b)

1. *His relationship to believers*

Three points about Him are made. *First,* He is the "Savior" *(sōtēra).* When Jesus was born, the angels announced to the shepherds: "For unto you is born this day in the city of David

---

[5]The pronoun *(hēmōn)* occurs at the very beginning of the sentence.
[6]It is a plural noun.

a Saviour, which is Christ the Lord" (Luke 2:11). He was not only the promised Savior for the Jewish people, but also for the entire Gentile world (John 4:42). This title is also a direct proof of the deity of Christ because the titles "God" and "Savior" are used interchangeably of the same divine being. Paul confessed that "we trust in the living God, who is the Savior of all men, specially of those that believe" (I Tim. 4:10). The Old Testament openly declared that only Jehovah could be the Savior of His people (Ps. 106:21; Isa. 45:21; 49:26). Since Christ bears the name of Savior, He must also be Jehovah God. Those two concepts are joined in this expression of hope: "Looking for that blessed hope, and the glorious appearing of the great God and our Savior Jesus Christ" (Titus 2:13).

Second, His full name is "Lord Jesus Christ." This is the name which every tongue will confess and before whom every knee will bow (2:10–11).

Third, He will come from the seat of our citizenship, namely, the Holy City within the heavens. The word "whence" *(hou)* is singular; therefore, its antecedent must be "citizenship" (singular), not the heavens (plural).

2. *The relationship of believers to Him*

Believers should "look" *(apekdechometha)* for Him because of who He is and what He has done.[7] The word "look" stresses an earnest longing, an eager expectation, and an anxious waiting. With such heightened anticipation, believers groan within themselves, "waiting [same word] for the adoption, to wit, the redemption of our body" (Rom. 8:23, 25). To those who "look [same word] for him shall he appear the second time without sin unto salvation" (Heb. 9:28).

C. Our Change Will Come from Him (3:21)

The present nature of the human body is suited to temporal life on this planet. It must therefore be changed in order to function in the eternal state (I Cor. 15:50). This change can

---

[7]The verb *(apekdechometha)* literally means "to receive out of from."

occur in one of two ways. *First,* if a believer is alive at the time of Christ's return he will be translated into a glorified body. *Second,* if a believer has died before Christ's coming his body will be raised from the dead and transformed into an immortal, incorruptible body (I Cor. 15:51–57).

1. The object of the change

The object of the change is "the vile body." This does not mean that the body per se is sinful. The literal translation is "the body of our humiliation." It refers to the mortal, corruptible body which was caused by the introduction of sin into the human race by Adam. It is thus subject to disease and to death. It is marked by dishonor and weakness (I Cor. 15:43). There is nothing more humbling than a diseased body hooked to a life-support system or a lifeless body in a coffin.

In such a body, Christ humbled Himself in order to die on the cross (2:8), and in the same type of body believers will one day die.

Christ will "change" this body at His return. The verb (*metaschēmatisei*) emphasizes outward appearance. Christ took the "fashion" (*schēmati*) of man. Although He was God incarnate, men saw Him only as a man. He took the appearance of man in order that He might change the appearance of man. Believers thus are promised that they will have new, immortal, incorruptible bodies, not subject to disease or death. The limitations of this body, as seen in the necessity of food and rest, will also be eliminated in the new body which is suited for eternity.

2. The goal of the change

When the change occurs, believers will "be fashioned like unto his glorious body." Elsewhere, Paul wrote: "As as we have borne the image of the earthy, we shall also bear the image of the heavenly" (I Cor. 15:49). John said that "we shall be like him; for we shall see him as he is" (I John 3:2). The God-man, Jesus Christ, today lives in a resurrected, glorified, immortal, incorruptible body. This body passed through the grave clothes, the stone tomb, and closed doors.

It had the capacity to eat and to drink, although there is no indication that the resurrected body will have to do so in order to sustain life.

The word "fashioned" (*summorphon*) means a "joint form." It refers to the inner essence of the new body. Believers will not become little gods nor will they look exactly like Jesus Christ or like each other. There will be no sin nature in this new body. It will be controlled by the spirit, not by the soul (I Cor. 15:44). Christ, who was in the form (*morphē*) of God, took the form of a servant in order that we might be conformed to Him throughout eternity.

3. *The guarantee of the change*

This change will be "according to the working whereby he is able even to subdue all things unto himself." The same divine power which enabled Christ to conquer death through His resurrection and which will enable Him to force all of His enemies into total submission is the same power which will change the bodies of believers. It is sovereign omnipotence which no one can resist. The resurrection change will happen because God has decreed that it will occur (cf. Dan. 4:35). God always does what He says He will do.

Questions for Discussion

1. Are Christians sometimes stubborn? In what areas? How can they be changed?

2. Why do evangelicals differ over the standards of the Christian walk? Can unity ever be achieved in this area?

3. How can we tell whether we should follow a human leader? If such leadership is not followed, is that disobedience?

4. Who are the enemies of the cross today? What are the means by which this judgment can be made?

5. From what things has Christ saved us? Do men restrict the application of salvation to certain areas of their life?

6. What should be the Christian approach to funerals? To cremation?

12

The Joy of Peace
Philippians 4:1–9

A modern beatitude states: "Blessed is the person who is too busy in the day to worry and too tired at night to do it." Some psychologists claim that only 8 percent of a person's worries are legitimate. They assert that 40 percent of such anxieties will never happen, that 30 percent are undue self-criticism, that 12 percent are about old decisions, and that 10 percent pertain to health and aging.

Problems inevitably will come to all people, including Christians. Job confessed: "Yet man is born unto trouble, as the sparks fly upward" (Job 5:7). Christ predicted future tribulation for His own, but He also promised the protection of His peace (John 14:27; 16:33). When a believer is controlled by the Holy Spirit, he will manifest both joy and peace (Gal. 5:22).

In this passage, Paul gave his final commands to the church. He wanted them to experience love, joy, and peace in three distinct areas.

I. IN HUMAN RELATIONSHIPS (4:1–3)

In these verses Paul addressed the church collectively (4:1), two women (4:2), and his coworker (4:3). In his remarks he revealed three aspects in which the joy of peace can be seen.

STAND UNITED IN JOY

A. Through Love (4:1)

The conjunction "therefore" *(hōste)* gives the logical result of both the explanation of salvation and the warning about the Judaizers (ch. 3).

1. Their description

Paul expressed his affection for the Philippian believers by five forms of address. *First,* they were his "brethren." They both had been born again into the family of God. He was their spiritual father, but still they were brothers. He regarded them as genuinely saved.

Second, they were "dearly beloved" *(agapētoi).* This description occurs twice in the verse, at the beginning and the end. He not only loved them because they were his brothers, but because he wanted to (I Thess. 4:9–10).

Third, they were "longed for" *(epipothētoi).* Earlier, he had expressed that he longed after them (1:8). He did not desire their money or support; rather, he wanted *them.* This adjectival title placed great emphasis upon an inner emotional longing.

Fourth, they were his "joy." Paul felt this way about all of his converts. Elsewhere he wrote: "For what is our hope, or joy, or crown of rejoicing? Are not even ye in the presence of our Lord Jesus Christ at his coming? For ye are our glory and joy" (I Thess. 2:19–20). He rejoiced in them personally, not just in what they had done for the Lord. Men today often rejoice over their business success or athletic victories to the neglect of their families. In the final analysis, the most important "thing" in the world is a person, a loved one. Real joy is rejoicing in people.

Fifth, they were his "crown" *(stephanos).* A victorious runner in the Greek games received a festive garland on his head (I Cor. 9:24–25). At the judgment seat of Christ, believers will receive different crowns for distinctive achievements (II Cor. 5:10). To the apostle, the Philippian believers represented the joy of victory because he knew that his race and labor in Philippi had not been in vain (2:16).

2. *Their defense*

Paul preceded his warning about the legalists with a command to rejoice in the Lord (3:1). He then defined the acceptable position as being found in the Lord (3:9). Now, the apostle issued an imperative to "stand fast in the Lord."

The admonition *(stēkete)* means to take a stand and to remain firm in that position.[1] He did not want them to yield to the pressures of the Judaizers. His personal testimony, which covered the breadth of divine salvation (justification, sanctification, and glorification), provided the church with adequate spiritual weapons to withstand the false attacks.

The location of their stand was to be "in the Lord." They had to relate everything to His divine-human person and to His redemptive death and resurrection. Their stand was not to be taken in a minor theological point or a denominational distinctive. They were to stand within their acceptable standing in the beloved Savior.

B. Through Unity (4:2)

1. *Objects of the appeal*

The two women mentioned here were the thorns in the apostle's crown (cf. 4:1). Since the apostle constantly encouraged unity (1:27; 2:2; 3:16), these women must have possessed great divisive influence upon others. Otherwise, why did he single out their names for emphatic, personal mention?[2]

Their real identity remains a mystery.[3] They may have been among the women who were saved when Paul first preached at Philippi; if so, they would have been two of the charter members of the church (Acts 16:13). If the church had two distinct assemblies, they may have met in the private

---

[1]It is a present verb actually based upon a perfect stem.

[2]Both names are stressed by occurring before their respective verbs. The name "Euodias" means a "prosperous journey"; the name "Syntyche" means a "pleasant acquaintance."

[3]The names occur only here in the New Testament.

homes of these two women. For this reason, some have suggested that one of the names was symbolic of Lydia, in whose house the believers first met (Acts 16:15, 40). Quite possibly they may have been deaconesses or women of financial wealth. In any case, the friction between these two women had to be eliminated.

2. Purpose of the appeal

To show no partiality, Paul used the same verb of appeal twice ("I beseech"). Both shared equal blame for their disgraceful conduct. The fact that the apostle criticized them in this public epistle shows that the entire church must have known about their personal conflicts. Apparently even the church was unable to resolve the problem.

Since men and women have distinctive personalities, there are bound to be differences of opinion. People have various tastes in food, clothes, and hobbies. In spiritual matters, however, there should be unity. Thus, Paul charged them to "be of the same mind in the Lord." Literally, they were to think the same thing (cf. 2:2; 3:16). Refusal to do so indicates a spirit of carnality and disobedience (3:15). No church or leader can have the joy of peace when members are bickering.

C. Through Help (4:3)

1. The giver of help

These women needed assistance to resolve their differences. Paul then made a personal request to a close friend to give such help. The verb "entreat" (erōtaō) suggests the equality of the one who is asked with the one who asked (cf. Luke 7:36). There is an obvious contrast between the firm appeal to the women ("beseech," parakaleō) and this gracious request ("entreat").

The identity of the "yokefellow" (suzuge) remains a mystery. Some assign the title to a woman, either Lydia or Paul's wife (Acts 16:14); however, the adjective "true" is masculine, not feminine. A few have suggested Epaphroditus; however, it would be strange for Paul to admonish him in the letter when he was with the apostle at the time of writing. The most plausible view is that the term should be seen as a proper name *(Suzugus)*. Names of other individuals are given in the context. Within the New Testament, no known person is given this adjectival description.[4] The addition of the adjective "true" *(gnēsie)* indicates that he was in character and conduct what his name meant. A *suzugus* was a crossbar with loops on the end through which the heads of two oxen were placed. Paul thus regarded Suzugus as a genuine coworker in the ministry.

The request was direct and simple: "Help them" *(sullambanou autais)*. The verb was used of seizing (Matt. 26:55), conceiving (Luke 1:24), and of taking hold together with someone (Luke 5:7). The verb prefix *(sun)* may indicate that others, perhaps Clement and the coworkers, were already trying to help them.[5]

2. The recipients of help

In spite of the present disunity of the two women, Paul still appreciated who they were and what they had done for the Lord in the past. *First,* they had "labored with [him] in the gospel." The verb *(sunēthlēsan)* was used earlier of "striving together" for the advance of the gospel (1:27). The apostle viewed the gospel outreach as a "coed" task in which believing men and women could team up together to reach the lost.

Second, their names were "in the book of life." They were definitely saved. This book contains the names of those who have received eternal life from God through faith in His gracious provision by Jesus Christ (Luke 10:20; Rev. 20:15).[6]

---

[4]Compare with fellow soldier or companion in labor (2:25).

[5]The prefix means "with"; thus, he was to give help with others.

[6]This is the only verse outside of the Book of Revelation where the Book of Life is mentioned.

The reference to Clement[7] and to the fellow laborers is probably a parenthetical thought. They also were part of the team, along with Paul and the women, which originally founded the church.

II. IN THE HUMAN HEART AND MIND (4:4–7)

Complaint and anxiety are the opposites of joy and peace. God wants His children to have the latter, but they must also want them so badly that they will do what the Bible says they must do in order to get them. The joy of inner peace will come automatically if the behavior follows the fivefold procedure given by Paul.

A. The Prerequisites of Peace (4:4–6)

1. Rejoice in the Lord always (4:4)

Paul admonishes the Philippians to be happy people. Nehemiah knew that "the joy of the Lord" was the strength of God's people. (Neh. 8:10). Solomon observed that "a merry heart" made a cheerful countenance and did "good like medicine" (Prov. 15:13; 17:22).

Constant rejoicing should be an integral part of the believer's inner response to life's pleasant *and* difficult situations. The repetition of the imperative twice ("Rejoice") and the use of the adverb ("always") prove that principle. Elsewhere the apostle wrote: "Rejoice evermore" (I Thess. 5:16).

The sphere of rejoicing must always be "in the Lord." A Christian should experience sorrow when a loved one is sick or dies. It would be wrong and contrary to wholesome human instinct for him to be happy at that time. Happiness can only occur when outward circumstances are pleasant, but inner joy can be present at all times. James commanded: "Count it all joy when ye fall into divers temptations" (James 1:2). The

---

[7]He should not be confused with Clement of Rome or Clement of Alexandria, two well-known men of later church history.

fruit of the Spirit-filled life is always joy, regardless of outward influences. A Christian can rejoice in the Lord because he knows that he is saved, that God cares, and that God is working out His sovereign plan for His glory and for the spiritual good of His people (Rom. 8:28).

2. Be gentle (4:5a)

The second prerequisite for inner peace is stated: "Let your moderation be known unto all men." The term "moderation" *(epieikes)* means gentleness, reasonableness, magnanimity, forbearance, good will, and a friendly disposition. A magnanimous person bears trouble calmly and rejects revengeful meanness.

Christ was both meek and gentle (same word) in His relationships with men (II Cor. 10:1). His gentleness, however, must not be confused with moral softness nor His meekness with authoritative weakness. The same Christ who beckoned the little children also drove the religious racketeers out of the temple with a scourge. Divine wisdom is "first pure, then peaceable, gentle [same word], and easy to be entreated" (James 3:17). Translated as "patient," it is one of the qualifications of a pastor (I Tim. 3:3).

This spirit of nonviolence must be manifested to "all men," both friends and enemies. Paul cautioned believers "to speak evil of no man, to be no brawlers, but gentle [same word], showing all meekness unto all men" (Titus 3:2). A believer must suffer wrong, but he should never initiate wrong (I Cor. 6:7). He must bless them which persecute him and must overcome evil with good (Rom. 12:14, 21).

Christ provides the perfect example of gentleness. On the cross, "when he was reviled, [he] reviled not again; when he suffered, he threatened not" (I Peter 2:23). He forgave His tormentors.

A person who retains spite is simply winding up the watch spring of his emotions for a breakdown. If he has no peace with God or man, he can never have inner peace. A gentle person, however, will be both a glad and a godly person.

3. Be alert to divine presence (4:5b)

In the midst of four imperatives (4:4–6), Paul inserted a promised truth: "The Lord is at hand." The presence or absence of inner peace will be in direct proportion to one's awareness of the presence of Christ. The expression "at hand" *(eggus)* refers to a nearness, either of time or space.

First, it could refer to the imminency of Christ's return (James 5:7–8). Paul had just discussed the blessed hope of the believer in which he will see Christ and receive a new body (3:20–21). If a Christian is looking up and ahead, he will not be depressed by looking down or back. Anxiety is often caused by an uncertain future, but a believer knows that he could be with Christ at any moment.

Second, it could refer to the omnipresence of Christ. He is not only in the believer, but also with him at all times and in all circumstances (Matt. 28:20). God is the constant environment of all of His children. A Christian is never alone, but when he thinks that God has deserted him he will become fearful. He must believe that God is where he is and that God can meet his every need. Hudson Taylor, the great missionary to China, confessed: "Counting Jesus as never absent is holiness evermore."

A hoping Christian will be both holy and happy. A sensitive believer will also be sane and sanctified.

4. Do not worry about anything (4:6a)

There is a difference between genuine care and false anxiety. Muller wrote: "To care is a virtue, but to foster cares is sin, for each anxiety is not trust in God, but a trusting in oneself, which comes to inward suffering, fears, and worry."[8]

The verb "be careful" and its noun "cares" are used throughout the New Testament in both a positive and a negative sense. *First,* Timothy had a constructive concern for the church (2:20). Paul knew that his associate would pray,

---

[8]Jac. J. Muller, *The Epistles of Paul to the Philippians and to Philemon,* p. 141.

witness, teach, and counsel effectively. The apostle himself asserted that the care of all the churches was upon him (II Cor. 11:28). He prayed for them, wrote to them, visited them, and sent his associates to them. Asking God and doing what he could formed a positive, loving care for others.

Second, a false care is self-destructive. Christ claimed that a person should not worry about the basic necessities of life which the heavenly Father has promised to provide (Matt. 6:25), about things that cannot be changed (Matt. 6:27), and about the problems of tomorrow (Matt. 6:34).[9] Such worry is caused by a lack of faith and by a wrong set of values and priorities (Matt. 6:30–33). Such cares, like weeds, choke the application of God's word to one's life and make one insensitive to the coming of Christ (Matt. 13:32; Luke 21:34). False cares should be cast upon the Lord because He genuinely cares for His own (I Peter 5:7; cf. Ps. 37:5; 55:22).

5. Pray about everything (4:6b)

The strong contrast between worry and faith is seen in the transitional adversative "but" *(alla).* A worrying Christian will waver, but a trusting believer will be triumphant.

Four concepts of prayer are set forth as the divine remedy for a troubled soul. *First,* "requests" *(aitēmata)* are specific petitions addressed to God. If a man needs wisdom, he should ask for it (James 1:5). *Second,* "prayer" *(proseuchē)* is the general invocation of God in which a believer gives his adoration, devotion, and worship. *Third,* "supplication" *(deēsei)* refers to the desperate cry for help arising from need. *Fourth,* all prayer must be accompanied by "thanksgiving." A believer must thank God for the answers in advance, for His loving concern, and for access into the divine presence through Christ's meritorious work.

Elsewhere Paul charged: "Pray without ceasing. In everything give thanks: for this is the will of God in Christ Jesus

---

[9]The English phrase "take no thought" is from the same Greek verb *(merimate)* translated as "be careful."

concerning you" (I Thess. 5:17–18). A believer must not only endure a trial, he must also thank God for it. When that occurs, he will have a positive approach to his problem, rather than negative worry and futility.

B. The Provision of Peace (4:7)

When a person has joy within, gentleness around, and prayer above, then he will experience peace.

1. *Its description*

First, it is "the peace of God." When a believing sinner has been justified by God, he possesses positional peace with God (Rom. 5:1). Christ thus becomes his peace (Eph. 2:14). In the world, however, he also needs the daily, practical application of the peace of God. It displaces the anxiety of men. Hendriksen described such peace as "the smile of God reflected in the soul of the believer."[10] Isaiah gave this Old Testament parallel: "Thou wilt keep him in perfect peace, whose mind is stayed on thee: because he trusteth in thee" (Isa. 26:3). It is divine peace in that its source is God and it manifests the attribute of His eternal being.

Second, it "passeth all understanding." It is totally foreign to the experience of the unsaved man. Even when a believer rests in its presence, he cannot verbalize what has happened. Christ said that His peace was different from that given by the world (John 14:27). Muller contended that it "excels and surpasses all our own intellectual calculations and considerations, all our contemplations and premeditated ideas of how to get rid of our cares."[11] The giving of this divine peace is just another proof that God always does "exceeding abundantly above all that we ask or think" (Eph. 3:20).

---

[10]William Hendriksen, *New Testament Commentary: Exposition of Philippians*, p. 196.

[11]Muller, *The Epistles*, p. 142.

2. *Its defense*

Three facts are set forth about divine peace. *First,* it will "keep" *(phrourēsei)* the believer. The derivation of this verb *(pro* and *horaō)* means to see before or to look out. It is a military term, used of a garrison of soldiers or sentries on duty. In that sense, Paul used the word for the governor of Damascus who kept the city with a garrison in order to apprehend the apostle (II Cor. 11:32). Just as soldiers of the praetorium guard were assigned to keep Paul under protective custody, so the peace of God can stand in constant vigilance over the child of God. The same verb is used of Christians "who are kept by the power of God through faith unto salvation ready to be revealed in the last time" (I Peter 1:5).

Second, the peace of God will patrol the "hearts and minds" of believers. The believer can enjoy emotional and mental stability if he rests in this divine protection. Modern homes are often guarded by dogs, watchmen, alarm systems, flood lights, and electronic gear so that the occupants can be undisturbed. In like manner, the peace of God can prevent anxiety from disrupting the feelings and thoughts of Christians.

Third, it will keep the believer "through [in] Christ Jesus." He must have both his position and practice in Christ. If he is disobedient or carnal, he cannot expect to have inner tranquility. Only he that "dwells in the secret place of the most High" can claim the promise of His peace (Ps. 90:1). He must abide in Christ and permit Him to manifest Himself through his inner life.

III. IN HUMAN ENDEAVOR (4:8–9)

Faith must lead to constructive action. Negative anxiety must be replaced by positive habits (cf. Eph. 4:25, 28–29). After praying, a believer must get involved in right thinking and doing. The two imperatives ("think" and "do") give these two apostolic directives.

STAND UNITED IN JOY

A. By Right Thinking (4:8)

The introductory words ("Finally, brethren") reveal the conclusion to this section.

1. Description of right thought

Six objects of right thought are listed. All are introduced by the qualitative adjective "whatsoever things" *(hosa)*. The plural indicates that many thoughts could be grouped under each category. Paul stressed here the object of thought rather than the fact of thought.[12] A well-known business has as its motto *THINK*. God, however, is more interested in *what* His people are thinking.

First, "true" things are the opposite of lies and false witness. A true issue is that which corresponds to the true nature of God (Rom. 3:4). A believer must surround his heart and mind with the girdle of truth (Eph. 6:14), he must produce the fruit of the Spirit in truth (Eph. 5:9), and he must speak the truth in love (Eph. 4:15, 25).

Second, the adjective "honest" *(semna)* comes from a verb which means to worship or revere *(sebō)*. Thus, honest thoughts are dignified and serious, prompted by holy morals and motives. Believers should desire to "lead a quiet and peaceable life in all godliness and honesty" (same word, I Tim. 2:2). Titus, pastors, and aged believers should be marked by such seriousness (I Tim. 3:4; Titus 2:2, 7).

Third, those things which are right in relation to God and man are "just" *(dikaia)*.

Fourth, "pure" *(hagna)* things are those which will not contaminate oneself or others. They are stainless and morally chaste.

Fifth, a pleasing thought is "lovely" *(prosphilē)*. It is ethically beautiful and attractive. It produces concord, peace, and rest.

---

[12]Indicated by the first position in the verse before the verb.

Sixth, wholesome, constructive thoughts are "of good report" *(euphēma).* They are the opposite of "filthiness, foolish talking, and jesting" (Eph. 5:4). They contain no immoral or sexually suggestive inuendo.

2. *Execution of right thoughts*

All of the above six thoughts are characterized by "virtue" and "praise." Wiersbe said, "If it has *virtue,* it will motivate us to do better; and if it has *praise,* it is worth commending to others."[13]

The imperative "think" *(logizesthe)* stresses the idea of a constant thought process. A believer must daily strengthen the moral integrity of his thought life. Solomon observed: "For as he thinketh in his heart, so is he" (Prov. 23:7). A popular axiom says:

> Sow a thought, reap an action.
> Sow an action, reap a habit.
> Sow a habit, reap a character.
> Sow a character, reap a destiny.

B. By Right Doing (4:9)

1. *The command*

The verb "do" *(prassete)* emphasizes constant practice, the development of a habitual lifestyle.[14] Paul wanted the Philippian believers to emulate him ("in me"). The church had a fourfold contact with the apostle, evidenced by the four verbal actions described. *First,* they "learned" from his oral instruction in their midst. He attempted to disciple them.

Second, they "received" truth as it was transmitted to them by way of this epistle and by his associates who had ministered to them.

---

[13]Warren W. Wiersbe, *Be Joyful,* p. 117.
[14]Present active imperative.

Third, they "heard" from others how Paul was responding to his Roman imprisonment. He was not anxious before the government authorities.

Fourth, they had "seen" Paul in action. They knew that he had prayed and praised God during his Philippian imprisonment. They knew from intimate acquaintance that the apostle practiced what he preached.

2. *The promise*

The believer has the guarantee that "the God of peace" will always be with him. He has the peace of God within him and the God of peace around him. He has both the presence and protection of peace, because wherever God is, so are His essential attributes.

Questions for Discussion

1. Are some Christian leaders more interested in programs than in people? What constitutes the joy of believers today?

2. When should a sinning Christian be rebuked publicly? Privately?

3. In what areas can women be effective laborers in the gospel? Should women take the place of men? Should they be ordained?

4. Are Christians sometimes vindictive? Why? How can this attitude be changed?

5. Why do believers worry? Should they go to psychiatrists? Christian psychologists?

6. How are our minds affected by TV? By contemporary music? By magazines and books? Should believers practice censorship?

13

The Joy of Financial Provision
Philippians 4:10–23

One major cause of anxiety is money—too much of it or too little. The rich worry about losing it and the poor worry about getting it. Money in itself is morally neutral; rather, it is the love of money which is the root of all kinds of evil (I Tim. 6:10).

Modern society too frequently and unfortunately has equated luxury with necessity. God, however, has only promised to provide us with our needs, not our desires. Christ assured His disciples that the heavenly Father would always supply food, drink, and clothing to His own (Matt. 6:25, 31). God provides, however, through human channels. In this section, Paul rejoiced in the faithfulness of God to meet his financial needs through the monetary gift sent to him by the church.

I. THE GIFT FROM PHILIPPI (4:10–20)

The church sent Epaphroditus as its messenger to give Paul some financial assistance. The return of the ecclesiastical servant afforded the apostle an opportunity to thank the church in writing.

A. His Attitude Toward the Gift (4:10–13)

1. He rejoiced in their renewal of interest (4:10).

Three observations are given. *First*, he "rejoiced in the Lord greatly" when he received their gift. Rejoicing is usually not self-initiated; rather, it is caused by someone or something.[1] He rejoiced because God had met his need and because God had constrained the Philippians to give. This same principle was designed to encourage the Corinthians to participate in the welfare collection (II Cor. 9:11-13).

Second, he recognized their personal interest in him. The phrase "your care of me" literally means "the act of thinking in behalf of me" *(to huper emou phronein)*. He was in their thoughts constantly.[2] Some people give without any thought of the people to whom they are giving, but this was not the case with the church. A popular axiom states: "Out of sight; out of mind." This was not so of them. In fact, the Philippian care for Paul "flourished." The verb "flourished" *(anethalete)* was used of trees and flowers which sprouted, shot up, and blossomed again in the spring after a dormant winter.

Third, he knew that they had wanted to give to him before this time ("wherein ye were also careful"). They simply had "lacked the opportunity" *(ēkaireisthe)* to do it. The verbal term means "no time" or "no chance." They did not know how they could get the money to the apostle. The trip of Epaphroditus to Rome thus gave them the opportunity.

2. He rejoiced in the lessons of contentment (4:11-12)

Paul stressed the fact that he did not rejoice over the amount of the gift ("not that I speak in respect of want").[3] He rejoiced more in their thoughtfulness than in their money. He was more grateful for the givers than for the gifts.

Paul then used three verbs to describe his total acceptance of his financial condition. *First*, he *learned* to be self-sufficient regardless of whether he had much or little. The verb "learned" *(emathon)* views all of his learning experiences as

---

[1]Indicated by the second aorist passive verb.

[2]Indicated by the present infinitive, *phronein*.

[3]The negative "not" *(ouch)* occurs at the very beginning of the verse.

a whole. It took both time and trials to perfect this inner conviction. The adjective "content" *(autarkēs)* is a compound word meaning "self" *(autos)* and "sufficient" *(arkeo)*. It means that he learned to manage his financial affairs properly. He controlled the money; he did not permit money or the lack of it to decrease the effectiveness of his ministry or the joy of his heart. He gave the same counsel to Timothy: "But godliness with contentment is great gain.... And having food and raiment let us be therewith content" (I Tim. 6:6, 8). Many Christians worry that they will not be able to pay their bills if they give their money to worthy causes; but Paul wrote: "And God is able to make all grace abound toward you; that ye, always having all sufficiency *(autarkeian)* in all things, may abound to every good work" (II Cor. 9:8).

Second, he *knew* "how to be abased" and "how to abound." He knew how to get along with little and also with much. He did not become depressed when he found himself "in weariness and painfulness, in watchings often, in hunger and thirst, in fastings often, in cold and nakedness" (II Cor. 11:27). The verb "abased" means to be humbled *(tapeinousthai;* cf. 2:8). It is often difficult for a person to accept gifts graciously from others. The apostle also knew how to use money when he had it. He did not become proud or complacent. Likewise, a rich Christian must learn how to ask God to give him his daily bread (Matt. 6:11).

Third, he was *instructed* to trust in God regardless of his financial circumstances. The verb *(memuēmai)* was used of the pagan mystery religions when a person was initiated into a secret society. The apostle thus was initiated into that group of believers who learned to put their confidence in God, not in gold. His faith in divine provision was not weakened by depression, recession, inflation, or affluence ("everywhere and in all things"). Food and money, in shortage or abundance, did not alter his spirituality.

3. *He rejoiced in the enablement of Christ (4:13)*

Paul's statement of confidence ("I can do") did not originate from egotistical pride. The verb *(ischuō)* stresses a strength of the will which controls the feelings and the body. The apostle knew that divine strength was made perfect through his human weakness (II Cor. 12:9). The more dependent upon God he became, the stronger he developed.

His strength came from his union with Christ ("through Christ which strengtheneth me"). Christ Himself said to the disciples: "... without me ye can do nothing" (John 15:5). The Savior enjoyed few material possessions on this earth. He had no place to "lay his head" (Luke 9:58). Women supported Him financially at times (Luke 8:3). He died, leaving only the clothes on His back. Likewise, Paul was supported by women in Philippi, and when he approached the end of his life he had to ask for his cloak (II Tim. 4:13). Christ thus did through Paul what He had achieved Himself.

B. His Evaluation of the Gift (4:14–20)

At first glance, the Philippians might have thought that Paul was not as grateful to them as he should have been. He had just announced how he could manage on very little financial support; however, he had not forgotten their human instrumentality. He was thankful to them, and he wanted them to know it. The conjunction "notwithstanding" thus served as the transition between divine sufficiency and human means.

1. He rejoiced over their present gift (4:14)

To them he said with thanksgiving: "Ye have well done." The adverb (kalōs) stresses that which is good and beautiful, an attractive appearance. All believers should desire to hear this praise from Jesus Christ: "Well done, good and faithful servant" (Matt. 25:23). When a person completes a task and does it well, he can then have a sense of personal satisfaction and internal joy (Gal. 6:4).

The explanation of their good work is given in the next phrase ("that ye did communicate with my affliction"). In Rome, the pressures came at Paul from all directions: the Roman authorities, the Judaizers, poorly motivated preachers, and the needs of the churches from which he had been absent for almost five years. The verb "communicate" *(sugkoinōnēsantes)* means fellow sharers or joint partakers. It is the basis of the popular concept of "fellowship." At the beginning of the epistle, Paul thanked the church for their "fellowship in the gospel from the first day unto now" (1:5). This involved the sharing of money as well as personal interaction.

2. *He rejoiced over their past gifts (4:15–16)*

He remembered two things which they had done for him during his second missionary journey (A.D. 49–52). This occurred about ten years before.[4] *First,* they had written to him about his financial needs after he left their city (4:15). He reminded them of this fact ("Now ye Philippians know also"). He especially noted what they had done shortly after they were saved ("in the beginning of the gospel"). The apostle had actively proclaimed the gospel for several years before he came to Philippi, but their city became the foundation for an evangelistic outreach into Europe, namely, the provinces of Macedonia and Achaia. The "beginning" therefore refers to their active participation in his ministry after they responded in faith. When he departed from Macedonia, he went into Achaia to the cities of Athens and Corinth (Acts 17:14–15). In correspondence with the Corinthians, Paul referred to the financial support of the Philippians:

> I robbed other churches, taking wages of them, to do you service.
> And when I was present with you, and wanted, I was chargeable to no man: for that which was lacking to me the brethren which came from Macedonia supplied (II Cor. 11:8–9).

Paul never asked for support, but he did not refuse it if it came unasked from outside sources. He never took money

---

[4]The first Roman imprisonment is dated A.D. 59–61.

from the people to whom he was presently ministering. Only the church at Philippi had "communicated" *(ekoinōnēsen)* or fellowshiped with him via letter, messengers, and gifts. By this time, other churches were in existence (Antioch in Syria, Antioch in Pisidia, Iconium, Lystra, Derbe); however, they did not expend the time or effort to discover what his needs were ("giving and receiving").

Second, they sent gifts on two different occasions ("once and again") during the month he ministered in Thessalonica (4:16). The apostle's next stop after Philippi was that neighboring Macedonian city. In this town, he again experienced "need," or a lack of funds for food and lodging. Their monetary gifts, however, permitted him to give more time to an evangelistic outreach, both in the synagogue and among the pagan idol worshipers (Acts 17:1–9; I Thess. 1:9).

3. He rejoiced over their future reward (4:17)

Paul was criticized for both his refusal to take money from one group and his willingness to accept it from others. When he labored in Philippi he did not take their money, but when he moved on to Thessalonica and Corinth he gladly received their support (I Thess. 2:3–8). He could not understand why his friends would entertain such attacks upon his integrity. He once wrote: "Have I committed an offence in abasing myself that ye might be exalted, because I have preached to you the gospel of God freely?" (II Cor. 11:7).

In the same manner, he now denied that he sought their money. The strong contrast between his negative and positive approach to money can be seen in the transition words: "not *(ouch)* . . . but *(alla)*."

The verb "desire" *(epizētō)* literally means "to seek upon." The apostle did not seek to add one gift upon another. They had already given to him twice; now he dispelled the notion that he was after a third, a fourth, and even more.

Rather, he sought after "fruit." He often referred to converts and to the righteous change within believing sinners as fruit (Rom. 1:13; 7:4; Eph. 5:9; Col. 1:6). In the parable of the sower and the seed, Christ gave this explanation of the good ground: "But he that received seed into the good ground is he that heareth the word, and understandeth it; which also beareth fruit, and bringeth forth, some a hundredfold, some sixty, some thirty" (Matt. 13:23). Fruit, for the believer, is total submission to the indwelling Christ who will then manifest Himself through the child of God (John 15:1–8). Just as Christ came to seek and to save the lost, so a fruitful believer will seek the salvation of others.

Paul did not want this fruit for himself but for them ("that may abound to your account"). This mercantile metaphor shows that the Philippians had made an investment in Paul's ministry which would bring them heavenly dividends. They were laying up treasure in heaven through him. Paul knew that they would be rewarded at the judgment seat of Christ for their financial support. Paul's converts were, in effect, their converts. Their gifts enabled him to evangelize more people.

4. He rejoiced over their sacrifice to God (4:18)

The apostle now looked at how their gift affected him and God. Three verbs are given to express its impact upon him. *First,* he received a full payment from them for his total investment of time in their lives. The verb "I have all" is a business term which speaks of total reimbursement. *Second,* he actually received more than he expected or deserved ("I abound"). The extra money was like a tip, over and above the actual cost. *Third,* he now was in a financial position without any immediate need ("I am full"). The verb indicates that his financial cup had been filled to the brim and that it had remained there up to the time of writing.[5] He did not need any more money from them.

He then described the gift which was sent by them through Epaphroditus, their messenger. He equated it with the sac-

---

[5]It is perfect passive indicative: *peplērōmai.*

rifices given to God by the nation Israel. Three aspects are cited. *First*, it was "an odor of a sweet smell." Israel presented to God five different offerings: burnt, meal, peace, sin, and trespass (Lev. 1:1–5:19). The first three were sweet-savour offerings, whereas the latter two were not. The first three were voluntary, given out of love, thanksgiving, and dedication; the latter two were compulsory, offered through confession of sin. The incense of the first three was sweet in the nostrils of God, but the latter two were not sweet. Thus their gift to Paul was voluntary, given out of love and gratitude.

Second, it was a "sacrifice acceptable." Paul commended the Macedonians for their welfare collection because they "first gave their own selves to the Lord, and unto us by the will of God" (II Cor. 8:5). Before God will accept and bless the financial gift of a believer, he must first present his body as "a living sacrifice, holy, acceptable unto God" (Rom. 12:1). Someone once wrote:

> Not what we give but what we share,
> For the gift without the giver is bare.

Third, their financial contribution was "well-pleasing to God." There is a difference between obeying the commandments of God and doing those things which are pleasing in His sight (I John 2:22). The former are required, but the latter go beyond the call of duty. Paul was pleased with their gift because God was pleased with it. The apostle also knew that the gift was really given to God even though he received the money.

5. He rejoiced over the sufficiency of God (4:19–20)

By making the apostle full, the church had created a financial need for themselves ("all your need"). They had poured out of the container of their lives into the vessel of Paul. He then informed them that God would fill them back up to the brim ("shall supply").[6] The verbs "supply" and "am full" come from the same Greek term *(pleroo)*. A person will always receive more than what he gave. God will make up the difference. Paul promised: "And God is able to make all grace abound toward you; that ye, always having all sufficiency in all things, may abound to every good work" (II Cor. 9:8).

Men may become impoverished when they give, but God can give out of inexhaustible wealth ("according to his riches in glory by Christ Jesus"). There is no end to His abundant provision for the needs of His children.

This promise, however, is restricted to those who create personal needs for themselves by giving to others.

Paul gave praise to God for meeting the needs of both the church and himself (4:20). He deserved the glory for that which had been done.

II. CLOSING REMARKS (4:21–23)

The epistle ended in typical Pauline fashion, with multiple greetings and a benediction.

A. Greetings (4:21–22)

1. From Paul

He saluted "every saint in Christ Jesus." He spoke to the entire church as a whole, but he now wanted to be remembered to each individual believer. Each Christian positionally is a saint, set apart from the world unto God by the initial sanctification of the Holy Spirit. Paul began the epistle with greetings to the saints (plural), and he now ends with greetings to each saint (singular).

---

[6]Note the personal relationship of Paul to God in the usage of the pronoun "my".

2. From the brethren

His associates ("The brethren which are with me") also wanted to greet the Philippians. This group probably included Timothy, Epaphras, Mark, Aristarchus, Demas, Luke (Philem. 23–24).

3. From the saints

The "saints" in Rome would include the membership of the church in that city (cf. Rom. 16:1–15). The greeting went from saints to saints. Both groups were one in Christ.

When Paul announced the greetings of the next group, the Philippians probably gasped in amazement. The Romans also wanted to greet them, "chiefly they that are of Caesar's household." Through the imprisonment of Paul, some servants, soldiers, and perhaps relatives out of the household of the emperor had been saved. This is why Paul could confidently assert that "the things which happened unto me have fallen out rather unto the furtherance of the gospel" (1:12). The church originally was saddened by news of his imprisonment; now he wanted them to rejoice with him over what God had accomplished in the lives of his captors.

B. Benediction (4:23)

Paul always magnified the grace of God. He wanted the church to experience the daily sustaining grace which all men need (John 1:16). Such grace is not restricted to just a few. So he wrote: "The grace of our Lord Jesus Christ be with you all." He began and ended with this theistic theme (1:2).

Questions for Discussion

1. How often should Christians give to the same missionary project? What often hinders such giving?

2. Have modern believers learned the secret of financial contentment? Have they succumbed to the pressures of business success, inflation, and material security?

3. What specific spiritual and financial problems does a wealthy believer encounter? A poor Christian?

4. What contrasts can be made between believers in the U.S.A. and those in underdeveloped countries? Between those who grew up in the Depression and this younger generation?

5. Should money management seminars be held in church? In what ways can the church assist its own in proper stewardship?

6. Have you ever written to a Christian college, a mission board, or an individual missionary to determine what their needs are? If not, why not? How can such lines of communication be improved?

7. How do Christians view their gifts of money? Do they really give to God or to the church treasury?

Selected Bibliography

Boice, James Montgomery. *Philippians.* Grand Rapids: Zondervan, 1971.

Hendriksen, William. *New Testament Commentary: Exposition of Philippians.* Grand Rapids: Baker Book House, 1974.

Lightfoot, J. B. *Saint Paul's Epistle to the Philippians.* Grand Rapids: Zondervan, 1953.

Martin, Ralph P. *The Epistle of Paul to the Philippians.* Grand Rapids: Eerdmans, 1976.

Muller, Jac. J. *The Epistles of Paul to the Philippians and to Philemon.* Grand Rapids: Eerdmans, 1972.

Pentecost, J. Dwight. *The Joy of Living.* Grand Rapids: Zondervan, 1973.

Strauss, Lehman. *Studies in Philippians.* Neptune, N.J.: Loizeaux Bros., 1959.

Wiersbe, Warren W. *Be Joyful.* Wheaton: Victor Books, 1975.